Forensic Science for Kids

Karen K. Schulz

Illustrated by David Parker

PRUFROCK PRESS INC.

WACO, TEXAS

Library of Congress Cataloging-in-Publication Data

Schulz, Karen K., 1962–
  CSI expert! : forensic science for kids / Karen K. Schulz.
    p. cm.
  ISBN 978-1-59363-312-7 (pbk.)
  1. Forensic sciences—Juvenile literature. 2. Criminal investigation—Juvenile literature. I. Title. II. Title: Crime scene
investigation expert!
  HV8073.S3464 2008
  363.25—dc22
                        2008003882

Edited by Lacy Elwood
Production Design by Marjorie Parker
Illustrated by David Parker

ISBN-13: 978-1-59363-312-7
ISBN-10: 1-59363-312-2

At the time of this book's publication, all facts and figures cited are the most current available; all telephone
numbers, addresses, and Web site URLs are accurate and active; all publications, organizations, Web sites, and
other resources exist as described in this book; and all have been verified. The authors and Prufrock Press make no
warranty or guarantee concerning the information and materials given out by organizations or content found at
Web sites, and we are not responsible for any changes that occur after this book's publication. If you find an error or
believe that a resource listed here is not as described, please contact Prufrock Press.

Prufrock Press Inc.
P.O. Box 8813
Waco, TX 76714-8813
Phone: (800) 998-2208
Fax: (800) 240-0333
http://www.prufrock.com

Dedication

This book is dedicated to my husband Jim, my son Matthew, and my daughter Taylor. The joy they bring to my life is immeasurable.

Contents

Acknowledgments

Special thanks to Dan Stoecklin, a Latent Print Examiner for the St. Louis County Police Department. Dan has shared his fingerprint expertise with my students for several years and was kind enough to give me a tour of the fingerprint lab.

I thank my wonderful husband, Jim, for giving me the encouragement I needed when I needed it the most. Thanks to my children, Taylor and Matthew, who are the most awesome kids you will ever meet. As the experiments were being revised for publication, they were willing to complete the labs and give me feedback from a middle school student's point of view.

Teacher's Guide

A variety of crimes, including robberies, arson, counterfeiting, computer fraud, and murder, are committed each day. Advances in science have allowed scientists to gather and analyze evidence from even the most minute piece of evidence. This study of evidence is called *forensic science*.

Students often are taught skills such as the scientific method, scientific research, critical thinking, making observations, analyzing facts, and drawing conclusions in isolation. Studying forensic science allows students to practice these skills and see theories put into practice by using circumstances that model real-life events.

A Note From the Author

When I first started teaching forensic science, there were limited resources available, so I created most of my own curriculum, including the *Crime Scene Detective* series. I do not have a science background nor do I have a classroom conducive to conducting experiments involving a variety of chemicals. I found that the forensic science experiment kits I ordered from various retail companies didn't come with step-by-step guides to help with the implementation of the experiments. They also used chemicals I didn't have access to or the experience of working with. I wanted to enhance my forensic science unit with hands-on experiences in processing and analyzing evidence, so over the course of several years I designed my own experiments that were age-appropriate, interesting, challenging for my middle school gifted students, and relatively easy to organize and conduct. This book is a compilation of those experiments. I've included very specific step-by-step directions for setting up and completing the labs so they easily can be used by teachers with limited science backgrounds.

Learning Objectives and Science Standards

By participating in these experiments, the learner will:

- study and apply the scientific method as it relates to a criminal investigation;

- recognize the role science plays in a criminal investigation;

- apply process skills such as critical thinking, deductive reasoning, observation, and comparative analysis;

- distinguish between relevant and irrelevant information;

- use logical reasoning to reconstruct events;

- communicate and defend a scientific argument;

- communicate valid conclusions;

- collect data by observing and measuring with precision;

- apply mathematical formulas;

- analyze and interpret information to construct reasonable explanations from direct and indirect evidence;

- organize, analyze, evaluate, make inferences, and predict trends from data;

- analyze, review, and critique scientific explanations, including hypotheses and theories, as to their strengths and weaknesses using scientific evidence and information;

- extrapolate from collected information to make predictions;

- collect, record, and analyze information using tools including metric rulers, hot plates, test tubes, microscopes, calculators, and field equipment; and

- become aware of careers associated with forensic science.

Interdisciplinary Topics

The study of forensic science is a multidisciplinary approach that has students actively involved in real-world experiences touching on information in a variety of content areas. Although the sciences are the primary content area, the students also will practice skills in math, language arts, art, social studies, and technology. Topics for the sciences include:

- Chemistry: fiber analysis, ink chromatography, chemical reactions.
- Earth Science: cast impressions.
- Life Sciences: anatomy (bones), fingerprints, blood, teeth.
- Physics: blood spatter patterns, glass fractures patterns.

Other curricular areas include:

- Mathematics: taking measurements, using formulas, trigonometry, solving word problems.
- Art: sketching crime scenes.
- Language Arts: oral and written communications, technical reading.
- Social Studies: criminal justice.
- Technology: computers, calculators, microscopes.

Grade Levels

These forensic science experiments were developed for a middle school gifted education class, but by adjusting the level of teacher involvement they easily could be used with grades 4–12.

How to Use the Experiments

This book contains experiments covering a variety of forensic topics. Each experiment has teacher instructions for gathering materials and setting up and implementing the lab and includes background research information. Most experiments also contain a student lab that includes a materials list, an essential question, background research, a crime fighting challenge that allows students to apply what they are learning in a real-world situation, and step-by-step experiment procedures.

The experiments are designed to be completed in stations so that the students can complete each lab by rotating through the stations independently or with a partner. The step-by-step instructions for students allow the labs to be completed with a minimal amount of help or direct involvement from the teacher. Several different labs may be set up in the room at the same time depending on the number of students you have and the amount of space available in your classroom. The background research included in the student labs provides basic information about the topic and, in some instances, gives more detailed information about the subject, drawing attention to the matter at hand. Including the background research allows the student to review previously learned knowledge, although in in some cases, it may be the initial exposure to the topic. The same background research also is included in the teacher instructions so that the teacher will have the basic information for each experiment available at his or her fingertips.

Although the majority of the experiments were designed to be completed independently by the students, some of the labs will require teacher instruction and demonstration. Instead of setting up lab stations in your classroom, you may choose to complete the labs together as a class.

Assessments

Student labs include a "Case Closed" section that requires students to draw conclusions and apply the information they have learned. These, along with the lab packets themselves, may be collected for a grade. A final test covering many of the topics also is included.

In addition, an answer key providing solutions to many of the student labs and worksheets is located on pages 138–143.

The Labs

I Spy: Documenting the Crime Scene
Teacher Instructions

This lab is teacher directed. No student lab procedures are needed.

Objective:

The student will examine and document evidence at a simulated crime scene.

Background Information:

Before forensic scientists can conduct experiments on potential pieces of evidence, the evidence first must be recovered from the crime scene. A crime scene must be searched carefully and thoroughly and documented in order to obtain all of the possible evidence and to help investigators reconstruct the events that occurred during the crime in order to solve the case.

There are several things that police routinely do at a crime scene. Typically, they first check the victim if there is one. They then secure the area by using a special type of plastic tape or ribbon that says "Police Line Do Not Cross." This tape is placed around the perimeter of the crime scene to deter unauthorized visitors from entering the area. The third step in the police procedures is to document the area by taking photographs or videos and/or making sketches. Measurements of the location of suspected pieces of evidence also are taken. Police continue to thoroughly search and document potential evidence. Witnesses also will be interviewed to gather additional information.

When officers acquire evidence at a crime scene, they follow a certain protocol to make sure the evidence is preserved and documented accurately and legally. Each piece of evidence collected is put into its own container. Depending on the type of evidence, it might be a plastic or paper bag. The container is then labeled and sealed. The label indicates where and when it was found and is initialed by the officer who found it. The evidence is then sent to the forensic lab. By following these procedures, police will have documentation proving when, where, and by whom the evidence was found. Police must be able to prove that the evidence was always in their possession.

Gathering Materials:

You will need to generate simulated pieces of evidence. You may want to create a fingerprint, a shoeprint, and a note, or any other type of evidence. Make orange cones out of construction paper, one for each piece of evidence you plan on having at the crime scene. Identify each cone with a letter, starting with "A." You will need tape measures and student copies of the Crime Scene Documentation: Evidence Location Chart on page 9.

Setting Up and Completing the Lab:

1. Create or gather the pieces of evidence you will place in your classroom to simulate a crime scene. You may include evidence like fingerprints, shoe prints, a handwritten note, and so on.

2. Place the evidence in various places in your classroom. Do this before students arrive to class.

3. When class begins, discuss the basic procedures for processing a crime scene as outlined in the background research.

4. Distribute the Crime Scene Documentation: Evidence Location Chart found on page 9.

5. Ask students to examine the crime scene without touching anything.

6. Next, students should sketch the crime scene (classroom) including major points of references such as student desks, computers, door, teacher's desk, tables, etc. They may sketch the room on the back of the Crime Scene Documentation paper.

7. As a class, discuss possible pieces of evidence seen in the room. Have students place the lettered cones next to each piece of evidence. For example, the fingerprint might be identified by the cone marked with a letter A, the shoe print by the cone marked with a letter B, and so on.

8. Students should then include in their drawings the items that the class has identified as evidence. They should place the letter that identifies the evidence in the appropriate location in the sketch, labeling each piece of evidence by the letter assigned to it.

9. Record these letters, a description, and the general location of the evidence in the appropriate places on the Crime Scene Documentation paper.

10. To better indicate the location of the evidence, have the students measure the location of each piece of evidence from two fixed points in the room. For example, if a note is located next to the trashcan that is near the door, students may measure the distance the note was from the classroom door and from a sidewall. The trashcan is an object that can be moved so it would not be considered a fixed object and should not be used when taking measurements. These measurements help put into perspective the rough sketch drawn by the student detectives.

11. Assign groups of students to measure and record a specific piece of evidence. Time permitting, you may rotate students through each piece of evidence so they can document more than one piece.

12. After students have finished processing the scene, discuss why it was necessary to follow certain procedures for searching the crime scene. Another topic for discussion might involve how investigators know if something is valuable evidence or just an item innocently present at the scene.

Special Notes:

If you have access to digital cameras or video cameras, you might want students to take pictures of the crime scene before taking measurements.

Name: _____ Date: _____

Crime Scene Documentation:
Evidence Location Chart

Date: _____ Time: _____ Location: _____

Letter	Description of Evidence and General Location	Description of Fixed Point 1 and Distance from Evidence	Description of Fixed Point 2 and Distance from Evidence
Example: A	Shoeprint on floor by teacher's desk.	Door frame left side—56 cm.	Outlet on back wall—34 cm.

Tool Time: Tool Impression Lab
Teacher Instructions

Objective:

The student will learn how tool marks are identified and used as evidence at a crime scene.

Background Information:

Most tools used at a crime scene will leave behind some kind of telltale mark called an *impression*. Impressions vary from scratch marks, to cut marks, to "jimmy" marks. Saws, wire cutters, or knives might leave cut marks, while a variety of tools might produce scratches when coming into contact with surfaces. A jimmy mark is the mark that is most often identified at a crime scene. You would most likely see this mark between a door and the door jam or a window and the windowsill. In this case, a tool such as a screwdriver or crowbar applies pressure until the door or window pops opens. Because the wood is "soft," an imprint of the tool is left behind.

Gathering Materials:

You will need four pieces of clay approximately 2 inches wide and 2 inches long. Three of the clay pieces should be of one color, while the fourth piece should be a different color. The fourth piece with the unique color will be the one used to make the impression of Exhibit A—the tool mark left behind at the crime scene.

You will need to get three flathead screwdrivers of similar style and size. They should not be exactly the same. For example, screwdrivers of similar size might have different markings on the screwdriver head. Some have heads with thinly spaced horizontal lines while some heads contain lines that are thick, and yet others (usually the cheaper brands) have no lines at all. When choosing the screwdrivers, pick three that are different but yet similar enough to require the students to look closely for unique identifying marks. Test the screwdrivers by making impressions on clay pieces to see what kind of impression they will leave behind. You also will need a magnifying glass, a metric ruler, and student copies of the Tool Time: Student Lab on pages 12–14.

Setting Up the Lab:

1. Make copies of the student lab on pages 12–14.

2. Flatten the four clay pieces into smooth, flat surfaces.

3. Label each screwdriver with a number from one to three. Writing the number on masking tape and wrapping it around the screwdriver handle works well.

4. Choose one screwdriver, lay the head of it on the uniquely colored piece of clay, and press down. You may need to experiment with the pressure you apply when making the impression. If you press too hard, the impression will be distorted. If you press too lightly, the impression won't be clear. This will be Exhibit A, the impression taken from the crime scene. Make a note of which screwdriver you used for later evaluation of student work.

5. Write Exhibit A on the bottom of a notecard and then place the clay with the impression you made in Step 4 on this card.

6. Determine where in the classroom the tool mark station will be and place the needed materials (three screwdrivers, three pieces of clay, Exhibit A, a magnifying glass, a metric ruler, and the students' Tool Time papers) at the station.

Special Notes:

Monitor students during the lab to make sure they are sketching and measuring correctly. Measuring in millimeters will give the most accurate measurement. Forensic scientists must summarize their findings in writing and students are asked to do the same for this lab.

Tool Time: Tool Impression Lab
Student Lab

Materials Needed:

Screwdrivers labeled #1, #2, #3; Exhibit A (clay with tool mark impression); three smooth, flattened clay pieces; magnifying glass; metric ruler.

Essential Question:

How can you determine which tool was used at the scene of a crime?

Background Information:

Most tools used at a crime scene will leave behind some kind of telltale mark called an *impression*. Impressions vary from scratch marks, to cut marks, to "jimmy" marks. Saws, wire cutters, or knives might leave cut marks, while a variety of tools might produce scratches when coming into contact with surfaces. A jimmy mark is the mark that is most often identified at a crime scene. You would most likely see this mark between a door and the door jam or a window and the windowsill. In this case, a tool such as a screwdriver or crowbar applies pressure until the door or window pops opens. Because the wood is "soft," an imprint of the tool is left behind.

Crime Fighting Challenge

At 5 a.m. on October 3, police were summoned to Marty's Diner. As Marty was entering his diner to prepare for the breakfast crowd, he noticed the back window in the storage room was broken. Upon further inspection, he realized he had been robbed. After the police questioned Marty, they identified three probable suspects: Eric, Kevin, and Joe. They also believe the window was pried open with a screwdriver. The police confiscated a screwdriver from each of the suspects. Follow the experiment procedures below to determine who was responsible for the break in at Marty's Diner.

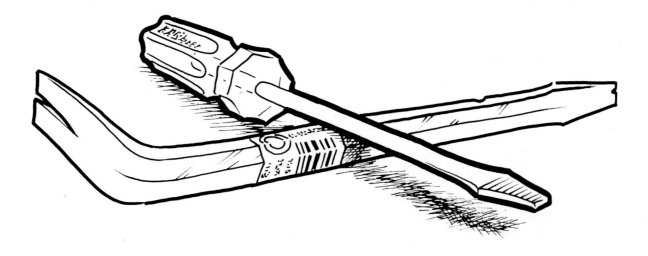

Experiment Procedures:

1. Using a magnifying glass, examine Exhibit A: a cast of the impression that was left at the broken storage room window. Take great care not to disturb the cast. You may look, but don't touch. Sketch the impression in the box below and then use the metric ruler to take measurements of the width of the tool. Record and label the measurements in millimeters. You may need to measure the impression in more than one place, for example, at the widest and narrowest places. Sketch in any unique marks or lines you see. In addition, write a description of what you see.

Exhibit A

Measurements: _____

Describe what you see: _____

_____

_____

2. Choose one of the three available screwdrivers. Make an impression of this tool by lightly pressing it into a piece of clay. (*Note:* Make sure the clay is smooth and flat before making your impression.) Sketch and measure in millimeters what you see. Repeat this procedure for the other two screwdrivers. (Sketch screwdriver #1 in the first box, #2 in the second box, and #3 in the third box.) In addition, write a description of what you see.

**Screwdriver #1
(Belonging to Eric)**

Measurements: _____

Describe what you see: _____

_____

_____

Screwdriver #2
(Belonging to Kevin)

Measurements: _____

Describe what you see: _____

Screwdriver #3
(Belonging to Joe)

Measurements: _____

Describe what you see: _____

_____

_____

CASE CLOSED

Compare the impressions from the suspects' screwdrivers to the impression left at the crime scene (Exhibit A). Based on your experiment results, which suspect is guilty? Justify your answer using specific information from your measurements and observations.

_____

_____

_____

_____

Crummy Cake Chemistry:
Chemical Analysis Lab
Teacher Instructions

Objective:

The student will learn how physical and chemical properties of an unknown substance can be used to identify the unknown substance and how it may be used in the study of evidence in a criminal investigation.

Background Research:

Forensic scientists often will receive physical evidence that is unidentified. For example, when looking at a powdery substance, police will not know right away if it is cocaine or another drug. When forensic scientists examine certain types of evidence, they look for properties of that evidence or substance that separate it from similar-looking substances.

Certain properties of an unknown substance may confirm it is evidence in a crime or the properties may rule it out as evidence. When examining a piece of evidence, scientists may study both physical and chemical properties.

Physical properties describe the evidence as it exists without it coming into contact with any other material. Chemical properties are used to describe the effects of the evidence coming into contact with another substance. In this lab, physical properties are used to describe how a mystery powder looks or feels. Chemical properties are used to describe what happens when the mystery powder comes into contact with water and with vinegar. In general, by understanding how a known substance will appear and how it will react when exposed to specific chemicals, scientists will be able to identify an unknown subject by comparing it and its reactions to that of a known subject.

Gathering Materials:

You will need three different containers filled with three different substances. The substances used in this lab are flour, cornstarch, and baking soda. The amount of each substance you need will be determined by the number of students you have completing the lab. Each group completing the experiment will need about 5 teaspoons of each substance. You will need six spoons, two for use with each powder. Each group of students will need six small paper cups and three pieces of black construction paper, approximately 4 inches by 6 inches in size. Water and vinegar also are needed, approximately 3 tablespoons of each liquid per group. Have a supply of paper towels handy in case of spills. Students will need a permanent marker or pen to use in labeling the cups. Although optional, a magnifying glass may be useful for students when examining the physical characteristics of the powders. Newspapers may be used to cover the work area to minimize cleanup. You will need to make student copies of the Crummy Cake Chemistry Student Lab on pages 17–21.

Setting Up the Lab:

1. Make copies of the student lab on pages 17–21.

2. Cover the lab surface with newspapers.

3. Fill three different containers with flour, baking soda, and cornstarch using as much powder as needed for the number of students completing the lab. Label the container of flour Mystery Powder 1. The baking soda should be identified as Mystery Powder 2, while the container filled with cornstarch will be Mystery Powder 3.

4. Fill one container with water and a second one with vinegar using as much liquid as is needed for the number of students completing the lab. Be sure to label each container of liquid appropriately.

5. Cut black construction paper into small sections (approximately 4 inches by 6 inches) so you have three for each group.

6. Place the containers of mystery powders, the containers of liquids, cups, spoons, a marker, a magnifying glass, and the paper towels at the chemical reaction station.

Special Notes:

You may substitute other powders (e.g., salt, sugar, baking powder) for the flour, baking soda, and cornstarch. Both baking soda and baking powder react with the vinegar by foaming, bubbling, and fizzing, which clearly separates them from the other powders. Be sure to include one or the other in the lab.

You may choose to fill each of the small cups with the mystery powders prior to the lab instead of asking students to do it as part of their lab preparations.

Crummy Cake Chemistry: Chemical Analysis Lab
Student Lab

Materials Needed:

Three containers, filled with three different mystery powders labeled 1–3; six empty cups; water; vinegar; spoons; three pieces of black construction paper; paper towels; marker or pen; a magnifying glass (optional)

Essential Question:

How can observations and chemical tests be used to identify unknown powdered substances?

Background Research:

Forensic scientists often will receive physical evidence that is unidentified. For example, when looking at a powdery substance, police will not know right away if it is cocaine or another drug. When forensic scientists examine certain types of evidence, they look for properties of that evidence or substance that separate it from similar-looking substances.

Certain properties of an unknown substance may confirm it is evidence in a crime or the properties may rule it out as evidence. When examining a piece of evidence, scientists may study both physical and chemical properties.

Physical properties describe the evidence as it exists without it coming into contact with any other material. Chemical properties are used to describe the effects of the evidence coming into contact with another substance. In this lab, physical properties are used to describe how a mystery powder looks or feels. Chemical properties are used to describe what happens when the mystery powder comes into contact with water and with vinegar. In general, by understanding how a known substance will appear and how it will react when exposed to specific chemicals, scientists will be able to identify an unknown subject by comparing it and its reactions to that of a known subject.

Crime Fighting Challenge

Taylor is the reigning Betty Crocker Bake-Off champion and was excited to be competing again in this year's competition. Food critics throughout the nation predicted she would win again. In what was reported as a major upset, Taylor's famous Upside Down Chocolate Caramel Cake came in last place. After the winners were announced, a heartbroken Taylor ate a piece of her cake, only to discover it tasted terrible. She determined it had an overabundance of baking soda. Taylor knew there is no way she could have mistakenly added too much baking soda. She remembered that earlier in the day, as she was preparing her cake, three of her most serious competitors, Allison, Lauren, and Emily, stopped by to chat. They each acted rather suspiciously, trying to distract Taylor from her work.

As head of security for the Bake-Off, you are trying to get to the bottom of the questionable cake. While interviewing the three women Taylor suspects, you notice each and every one of them had a vial containing a white powder tucked away in their aprons. You know contest rules clearly state all cooking ingredients must be regulation and are provided by the Betty Crocker Company. Clearly in violation of contest rules, you confiscate the vials from each woman and take them back to the lab to identify the mysterious powders.

Follow the experiment procedures below to identify which of the three ladies was illegally carrying the concealed baking soda and is therefore the main suspect in this Case of the Crummy Cake.

Experiment Procedures:

1. Prepare your materials by labeling the small cups. Write each of the following labels on a different cup "1W," "1V," "2W," "2V," "3W," and "3V." (*Note:* The "W" stands for water and the "V" stands for vinegar.)

2. Place one teaspoon of Powder 1 into the cups marked 1W and 1V and return the spoon. Repeat this for each of the other powders, placing one teaspoon of Powder 2 into the cups marked 2W and 2V, and one teaspoon of Powder 3 into 3W and 3V. Be sure to use a different, clean spoon for each substance to avoid cross-contamination.

3. You will first examine the physical characteristics of the mystery powders.

4. Spoon out a small amount (about half of a teaspoon) of powder from the original Powder 1 container onto a sheet of black construction paper. (Make sure you use the spoon designated for Powder 1.) Carefully examine the appearance (including color) and texture of the mystery powder. Feel free to touch the sample that is on the paper and to use a magnifying glass to get a closer view. Record your observations in Table 1: Physical Properties.

5. Repeat this procedure with the other two powders using a new sheet of paper and a clean spoon each time. To avoid having powder residue on your fingers, be sure to wash or wipe off your hands between examining samples.

6. Now take a look at two chemical reactions. You will use water for the first reaction.

7. Using a clean spoon, pour 3 teaspoons of water into cup 1W and stir the mixture. Describe what you see, writing your answer in Table 2: Chemical Reactions. Pay attention to any changes in water color, texture, or residue that may remain in the cup. Wait a few minutes and then check the cup again to note any changes from your previous observations. Has the mystery powder completely dissolved or has it sunk to the bottom of the cup? Note any additional observations in Table 2.

8. Repeat this procedure with the other powders using cups 2W and 3W.

9. For the second reaction test, use vinegar.

10. Using a clean spoon, pour 3 teaspoons of vinegar into cup 1V and stir the mixture. Describe what you see in Table 2: Chemical Reactions. Pay attention to any changes in liquid color, texture, or residue that may remain in the cup. Wait a few minutes and then check the cup again to note any changes from your previous observations. Has the mystery powder completely dissolved or has it sunk to the bottom of the cup? Note any additional observations in Table 2.

11. Repeat this procedure with the other substances using cups 2V and 3V.

12. When you have completed the chart, ask your teacher for the Physical and Chemical Properties: Tables 3 and 4. Using these and your own test results, determine the identity (baking soda, corn starch, and flour) of each substance.

CASE CLOSED

Identify the mystery powder that each woman was carrying. Based on your experiments and the information on the physical and chemical properties tables, explain how you determined who was illegally carrying the concealed baking soda and sabotaged Taylor's Upside Down Chocolate Caramel cake.

_____

_____

_____

_____

_____

_____

_____

Crummy Cake Chemistry: Data Tables

Mystery Powder 1 was taken from Lauren.
Mystery Powder 2 was taken from Allison.
Mystery Powder 3 was taken from Emily.

Table 1: Physical Properties

Mystery Powder	Appearance/Color	Texture
Powder 1		
Powder 2		
Powder 3		

Table 2: Chemical Reactions

Mystery Powder	Reaction to Water	Reaction to Vinegar
Powder 1		
Powder 2		
Powder 3		

Table 3: Physical Properties of Known Substances

Mystery Powder	Appearance/Color	Texture
Baking Soda	Bright white, powdery	Silky, fine powder
Corn Starch	White, fine powder	Fine powder
Flour	Off-white, flat—no shine	Silky, any lumps can easily be flattened

Table 4: Chemical Reactions of Known Substances

Mystery Powder	Reaction to Water	Reaction to Vinegar
Baking Soda	Appears to dissolve, water turns milky white, cloudy, residue left at bottom after passage of time	Fizzes and bubbles up, foamy, white in color, residue left at bottom after passage of time
Corn Starch	Dissolves and thickens, water turns white and becomes pasty	Dissolves and thickens, vinegar turns white and becomes pasty
Flour	Thickens, air bubbles form when stirred, looks like pancake batter	Thickens, air bubbles form when stirred, looks like pancake batter

Check It Out: Counterfeit Check Lab
Teacher Instructions

Objective:

The student will learn about the safety features contained on a check and how to identify counterfeit checks.

Background Research:

A check contains many features that ensure it is processed through the correct bank account, that it is a real check, and that would deter possible counterfeiters. Carefully read the Check Out This Check handout to learn more about these features.

Gathering Materials:

You will need an authentic check and a color copy of the check. Copy the front side only. It is best to use a check from an account that is no longer open. If you have closed a checking account without using all of the checks, those checks would be ideal to use. You also may visit a local bank to see if they would give you a starter set of checks to use. If possible, use three or four checks to allow more students to work at this lab at the same time. You will need to make a color copy of each of the real checks.

The safety features are best viewed through a microscope. If you don't have a microscope, check with your science teachers to see if you can borrow one. A magnifying glass can be used if microscopes aren't available, however, it will be difficult to see the microprinting on the signature line.

Setting Up the Lab:

1. Make copies of the Check It Out Student Lab (pp. 24–26) and the Check Out This Check handout (p. 27). You do not need individual copies of the Check Out This Check handout. Just make a few to be used at the counterfeit check station.

2. Make color copies of the real checks you will be using.

3. As a precaution, write the word "VOID" on the checks in small enough print to allow students to observe the various safety features on the check.

4. On the authentic check, directly above the "Pay to the Order of" line, erase a section of the check as if someone had tried to erase an existing name. A white area should appear.

5. Paper clip the real check together with its matching color copy.

6. Place the checks and the microscopes or magnifying glasses at the experiment station.

Special Notes:

Although the concepts in this lab are basic, most students are fascinated by the concept of the microprinting on the signature line. Different check companies write different words on the signature line. One company might print "Authorized Signature" while yet another might write its name such as "MBNA AMERICA." If possible, use checks from different sources so the students can see the variety of printed words. It is almost impossible to see the lettering without the use of a microscope.

If you have access to extra checks, you may want students to experiment with making erasures on the checks so they can see how the chemical protection turns the erasure white.

Check It Out: Counterfeit Check Lab
Student Lab

Materials Needed:

Authentic check, color copy of check, microscope or magnifying glass, Check Out This Check handout

Essential Questions:

What safety features are included on a check? How can a person determine if a check is counterfeit?

Background Research:

A check contains many features that ensure it is processed through the correct bank account, that it is a real check, and that would deter possible counterfeiters. Carefully read the Check Out This Check handout to learn more.

Crime Fighting Challenge

A string of counterfeit checks have been passed in the area. The local police department has decided to put on a workshop for small business owners informing them about detecting counterfeit checks. You have been hired as a consultant to the police to teach the business owners about the safety features on checks. Follow the experiment procedures to learn more about counterfeit check detection.

Experiment Procedures:

Read the Check Out This Check handout. Use the microscope or magnifying glass when necessary to examine the real check. Answer the following questions. (*Note:* The real check will have printed information on the back of the check.)

1. Feel the edges of the check. Where does the perforation exist (top, side, bottom)? How can you tell?

_____

_____

2. Use a microscope or magnifying glass to examine the background on the front of the check. You should see little dots or lines. What is the purpose of these laid lines?

_____

_____

3. Study the signature line. Although this appears to be a straight line it is really a series of letters. Can you make out the words? You will need to use the microscope to see them. Write the words found in the signature line here.

_____

_____

4. Look at the "Pay to the order of" line. What could have caused the white area above the line to appear?

_____

_____

5. When viewed under normal lighting conditions, what would be the appearance of the magnetic ink (the numbers) on this real check?

_____

_____

6. Study the back of the check. List the safety features that are described.

_____

_____

Examine the color copy of the check. Answer the following questions.

7. Feel the edges of the check. Where does the perforation exist (top, side, bottom)? How can you tell? What does it mean if you can't feel a perforation?

_____

_____

8. Study the signature line using a microscope or magnifying glass. Can you make out any words? What happens to the appearance of the signature line on the copied check? (Describe what it looks like.)

_____

_____

9. When viewed under normal lighting conditions, what would be the appearance of the magnetic ink (the numbers) on this copied check?

_____

_____

10. Examine the background of the front of the copied check. How does this compare to the background of the real check?

_____

_____

CASE CLOSED

After reviewing check safety features, you are now ready to give advice to the group of small business owners. Describe what you believe are the three most important safety features for them to know. In other words, if they receive a check for future payment, what three things should they do or look for to make sure that the check is not counterfeit?

_____

_____

_____

_____

_____

_____

Check Out This Check

A

ERNEST P. WORREL		0001
512-555-1234	Date _____	
300 VARNEY WAY		
VERNON, MO 65712		

Pay to the
order of _____ $ [_____]

_____ Dollars

FIRST
National Bank   123 MAIN STREET
                 VERNON, MO 65712

For _____   _____

⑊083456790⑊ ⑈123456789⑊ 0001

B   **C**   **D**

E AUTHORIZED SIGNATURE ONLY

Here are a few features found on a check.

- **Perforations (See letter A above):** Most checks will be torn from a checkbook and will have perforations either on the top or on one side of the check. You should be able to feel the perforations when running your finger over the edge of the check. The edge will be "bumpy" or "jagged."

- **Routing numbers (See letter B):** The routing number identifies the bank at which the check should be processed. The first two digits indicate in which Federal Reserve Bank District the bank is located (08—Missouri in this case).

- **Personal account number (See letter C):** This number identifies the personal account of the individual who owns the checks. The last digits are the same as the check number (0001).

- **Magnetic ink (See letter D):** The numbers on a check are printed with special ink that allows machines to read and sort them during processing. When you look at the check under normal lighting conditions, the printed numbers look dull or flat. If the numbers look shiny, it is a counterfeit check.

- **Microprinting (See letter E):** The signature line is made up of small words that are not visible to the naked eye. The words are only visible on an original check when looking through a microscope. When a check is copied, the words appear as a blurry line because the individual letters are too small to copy clearly.

Other features include:

- **Chemical protection:** With chemical alteration, spots or stains will appear on the check. If a part of the check is erased, it will turn white.

- **Laid lines:** The background of the check contains unevenly spaced parallel lines (or sometimes dots). This makes it hard to cut and paste parts of the check because the lines are difficult to align correctly after cutting.

Take a Bite Out of Crime: Dental Impressions Lab
Teacher Instructions

Objective:

The student will learn how a dental impression may be matched to a suspect or victim.

Background Research:

Forensic odontology uses the principles of dentistry to identify human remains and bite marks. Forensic odontologists may use teeth and bite marks or impressions to help identify an unknown person. Like fingerprints, each person has a unique set of teeth. The alignment of the teeth, fillings, and chipped teeth are some of the characteristics that an odontologist will examine to help match a set of impressions or teeth to a suspect or victim. Dental records such as x-rays may play an important part in the identification process. The age of an unknown person also may be estimated by the number and type of existing teeth.

Gathering Materials:

You will need something in which students may leave a dental impression. Wedges of foam plates work well. Magnifying glasses and metric rulers may be helpful for students in examining the impressions. Student copies of the Take a Bite Out of Crime Student Lab on pages 30–31 also are needed.

Setting Up the Lab:

Part I. Making the Impressions

1. Make copies of the student lab on pages 30–31.

2. If using a foam plate, cut the plate into pie-like wedges. Cut enough of the pointy part of the wedge off so the student can comfortably bite down on the wedge. You will need two wedges for each student.

3. For Part I of the lab, distribute two wedges per student. You can give students the dental lab handout and ask them to follow directions or complete the activity as a class. In either case, follow the directions on the student lab.

4. After students have made their impressions, they should write their name on the outer edge of both pieces. Collect both pieces from each student. (You may want to ask the students to dry off the pieces before collecting them.)

Part II. Matching the Impressions

1. You will need to prepare the pieces for the second part of the lab. Take each pair of impressions and cut the name off of one of the wedges. Randomly assign a number to the wedge that no longer has a name. Write the number somewhere on the wedge so that it doesn't interfere with the bite mark pattern. On a separate sheet of paper, record the student's name and the number assigned to that student. Repeat this for all pairs of impressions.

2. Depending on the number of students you have, put the impression pairs into different groups. For example, if you have 24 students, you may want to divide the impressions into four groups of six pairs of impressions. Just make sure that you include the matching impressions in the same group. Store the groups of impressions in different plastic bags.

3. On the day you resume the lab, put the students into smaller groups. Give each group a bag filled with a set of the impressions and ask them to follow the procedures as given on their lab paper. You may ask students to compare all groups of impressions or just do one set.

Take a Bite Out of Crime: Dental Impressions Lab
Student Lab

Materials Needed:

Two pieces of Styrofoam, dental impressions made from Styrofoam, magnifying glass, metric ruler

Essential Question:

How can you match a dental impression to a suspect?

Background Research:

Forensic odontology uses the principles of dentistry to identify human remains and bite marks. Forensic odontologists may use teeth and bite marks or impressions to help identify an unknown person. Like fingerprints, each person has a unique set of teeth. The alignment of the teeth, fillings, and chipped teeth are some of the characteristics that an odontologist will examine to help match a set of impressions or teeth to a suspect or victim. Dental records such as x-rays may play an important part in the identification process. The age of an unknown person also may be estimated by the number and type of existing teeth.

Crime Fighting Challenge

Identifying bite marks often is vital in solving a crime. In fact, a majority of the time, unidentified victims may be identified by the use of teeth impressions. Use your investigative skills to correctly match a variety of bite mark impressions.

Experiment Procedures:

Part I. Making the Impressions

1. Choose a wedge of Styrofoam.

2. Slip the narrow end of the wedge into your mouth so that it fits comfortably.

3. Bite down firmly on the wedge and then remove.

4. Repeat this procedure with a second wedge.

5. Write your name on both samples at the wide end of the wedge. Write your name on the side that represents the impressions of your top teeth.

6. Place both wedges in the location designated by your teacher.

This completes the first part of the experiment. The second part involves matching prints from your classmates. This will need to be completed after your teacher has processed the samples. Save this lab paper until that time.

Part II. Matching the Impressions

1. You will be examining two groups of dental impressions. Group 1 is identified by student name and Group 2 is identified by number.

2. Examine the impressions from each group looking at particular characteristics such as tooth position, width of bite mark, etc.

3. When you have determined which sets are matches, write the information in the table below. (*Note:* You may not need to use all of the rows.)

Name on Impression From Group 1	Corresponding Number on Impression From Group 2

CASE CLOSED

Choose one pair of dental impressions that you examined, identify the owner and the number of the impression, and then describe the unique characteristics that allowed you to match it to its corresponding impression.

_____

_____

_____

_____

_____

_____

Burn, Baby, Burn:
Fiber Identification Lab
Teacher Instructions

Objective:

The student will identify fibers by performing burn tests.

Background Research:

Fibers may be classified as either natural or synthetic. Natural fibers come from a plant or animal. Fibers also may be created by chemically altering raw materials. These fibers are called synthetic or artificial fibers. To identify an unknown fiber, a burn test may be performed. All fibers burn, but they react to fire in unique ways. When placed next to a flame, some fibers will flare up and burn right away, while other fibers may curl up, shrink, or melt. Some fibers will only burn while in the flame and will extinguish as soon as they are removed from the flame. Different fibers will present different ashes. Some fibers will produce ash that is fine and soft while others will produce a hard bead. The odor of burning fibers also will vary. You may detect the scent of burning wood, paper, or leaves, or it may smell sweet. Burning fibers also will produce different colors of smoke. Scientists who examine fibers are able to determine what type of fabric they are working with based on these various characteristics. If a fiber was found at a crime scene or on a victim, investigators may be able to use information about the fiber to link a suspect to the crime.

Gathering Materials:

A variety of fibers or fabrics are needed for this lab. Some science supply companies sell fiber kits but fabric swatches also will work. In fact, the fiber strands burn so quickly, it is often difficult to see what happens. Fabric swatches tend to burn longer and may be purchased at a local fabric store. This lab describes the use of fabric swatches and not strands of fiber. The fabrics recommended for this lab are cotton, polyester, rayon, acetate, acrylic, and nylon but other fabrics may be used. It is best to use fabrics that are not blended. You will need metal pie tins, tealight candles, and matches. Sealable plastic bags (snack size) are needed for storing the fabric samples, and tweezers are used for holding the fabric during the burn test. You also will need student copies of the Burn, Baby, Burn Student Lab on pages 36–39.

Setting Up the Lab:

1. The instructions given are for groups of students performing the experiment using fabric swatches. If you are demonstrating the lab, you only need to prepare one set of materials. If you are allowing the students to perform the lab, you will need a set of materials for each group of students.

2. Make copies of the Burn, Baby, Burn Student Lab on pages 36–39 and the Fiber Identification Chart on page 35.

3. Take one sample of fabric and cut it into small strips approximately ¼ of an inch wide by 1½ inches long. You will need two samples of the same fabric for each group to allow them to repeat the burn test. Put two of the fabric samples into a snack size resealable plastic bag and label the bag, "Sample A." On a separate note sheet, for your own record keeping, identify the type of fabric that is Sample A. Fill enough plastic bags for each group of students to have one. (If you are having students rotate through stations, you may place one bag at each station, filling the bag with enough of the swatches to accommodate the entire class.)

4. Repeat Step 3 for each type of fabric you are testing. Don't forget to label the bags (Sample B, Sample C, Sample D, etc.) and to make a note of which type of fabric is in each bag.

5. For each station or group of students, you will need an area to safely burn the fabric. Place a tealight candle into a tin pie plate. Fill the pie plate with just enough water to cover the bottom of the pan, being careful not to submerge the candle.

6. Place tweezers and the bags containing the fabric samples at each station.

7. Before beginning the lab, go over safety measures with the students. Some safety measures to include are:

   a. Never hold the fabric sample with your fingers. Always use the tweezers.

   b. Never place your hand or the tweezers directly above the candle, as the flames will rise when the fabric is lit. Expose the fabric to the flame by bringing it in from the side of the candle.

   c. Do not touch the end of the tweezers immediately after burning the fabric sample, as it will be hot.

   d. After burning a fabric swatch, place the end of the tweezers exposed to the flame in the water in the pie tin. This will cool off the tweezers so you can remove the remnant.

   e. In the event that a fabric burns out of control, drop the fabric into the water in the pie tin.

8. Light each candle when you are ready to have students begin the lab.

9. When students have completed all of the burn tests and filled out their Fiber Burn chart, give them a copy of the Fiber Identification Chart on page 35.

Special Notes:

Students who are careful and mature by nature should be able to safely complete the lab. Monitor the students closely while they are completing this lab.

Because this lab involves the use of an open flame, you might choose to just demonstrate the lab instead of allowing the students to perform the tests. If students will be completing the lab, demonstrate the use of the materials, especially the proper way of inserting the material into the fire. Be sure to emphasize all safety measures.

Your burn tests may vary slightly if you use a blend of fabrics. Perform the burn test with the samples you have and alter the fiber burn chart as necessary. One of the fabric samples you choose must be cotton, because cotton was identified at the crime scene.

Fiber Identification Chart

Burn Characteristics

Fiber	Reaction When Close to Flame	Reaction When in Flame	Color of Smoke	Odor
Acetate	Melts, curls up, shrinks away	Ignites, continues to burn when removed from flame	White smoke	Burning wood
Acrylic	Melts, curls up, shrinks away	Ignites, sputtering flame, dies out when removed from flame	Black smoke	Bitter
Cotton	Ignites immediately	Ignites, large flames, may flare up, continues to burn when removed from flame	No smoke when burning, gray smoke when fire burns out	Burning paper
Nylon	Melts, curls up, shrinks away	Difficulty igniting, dies out when removed from flame	White smoke while burning	Burning plastic
Polyester	Melts, curls up, shrinks away	Burns quickly, self-extinguishing	Black smoke while burning	Sweet
Rayon	Ignites immediately	Burns quickly with no flame or melting, continues to burn when removed from flame	No smoke	Burning leaves

Burn Baby Burn:
Fiber Identification Lab
Student Lab

Materials Needed:

Fabric samples, tweezers, burning candle in pie tin filled with water

Essential Question:

How can an unknown fabric be identified through the use of a burn test?

Background Research:

Fibers may be classified as either natural or synthetic. Natural fibers come from a plant or animal. Fibers also may be created by chemically altering raw materials. These fibers are called synthetic or artificial fibers. To identify an unknown fiber, a burn test may be performed. All fibers burn, but they react to fire in unique ways. When placed next to a flame, some fibers will flare up and burn right away, while other fibers may curl up, shrink, or melt. Some fibers will only burn while in the flame and will extinguish as soon as they are removed from the flame. Different fibers will present different ashes. Some fibers will produce ash that is fine and soft while others will produce a hard bead. The odor of burning fibers also will vary. You may detect the scent of burning wood, paper, or leaves, or it may smell sweet. Burning fibers also will produce different colors of smoke. Scientists who examine fibers are able to determine what type of fabric they are working with based on these various characteristics. If a fiber was found at a crime scene or on a victim, investigators may be able to use information about the fiber to link a suspect to the crime.

Crime Fighting Challenge

Christine James reported a fire in the east end of an abandoned warehouse on Fifth Street. The fire was quickly put out before it spread to the west end of the building and after examining the scene investigators ruled the fire an arson. Investigators found small fibers caught on a broken window on the west end of the building, which they believe to be the point of entry for whoever started the fire. The fibers left on the window were later processed and identified as cotton. At the time of the fire, investigators interviewed people who just happened to be at the scene. Police thought that several people were behaving rather strangely and wondered if they had anything to do with the fire. Police asked six people to come into the station for further questioning. A fabric sample from the shirt of each suspect was taken. Police believe that whoever was wearing cotton would be their prime suspect in this case of arson. Follow the experiment procedures to determine who was wearing the cotton shirt.

Experiment Procedures:

Caution: This lab involves the use of an open flame and burning fabric samples. Please follow the safety rules as discussed by your teacher:

Use the following steps to complete this experiment.

1. Look at the Fiber Burn Chart. You will be burning fabric samples and watching how the fabric responds to being near a flame and in a flame, and the color of smoke and odor it produces. Watch carefully for each of these items as you perform the experiment. (*Note:* You will fill in the last column "Identity of Fabric" after completing all experiments.)

2. Choose a fabric swatch from the plastic bag marked Sample A.

3. Place the fabric piece in the tweezers so that only a small portion is in the tweezers. *Caution:* Do not put the fabric into the flame by holding on with your fingers. You must use the tweezers.

4. Bring the fabric slowly over or near (but not into) the flame of the candle and observe what happens.

    a. Did it ignite right away?

    b. Did it curl up, shrink, or melt?

5. Record your results in the Fiber Burn Chart provided.

6. Now slowly bring the fibers into the flame and as soon as it catches on fire remove it. Observe what happens.

    a. Did it catch on fire immediately?

    b. When you removed it from the flame, did it go out or continue to burn?

    c. Did it produce any smoke when it burned? If so, what color?

    d. Did the smoke have an odor? Did it smell bitter, sweet, or like burning paper? How else might you describe the smell?

7. Record your results in the Fiber Burn Chart provided.

8. Repeat Steps 1–7 with the second fabric piece of Sample A. Repeating the procedure with the same fabric swatch gives you the opportunity to make

observations again and to look for characteristics (smoke color, odor, etc.) you may have missed when burning it the first time. Record any additional observations in the Fiber Burn Chart.

9. Once you've burned Sample A twice, repeat Steps 1–8 with the other five fabric samples. Be sure to record your observations in the chart provided.

10. After having burned all six fabric samples, identify each type of fabric. Ask your teacher for the Fiber Identification Chart handout, which identifies the burn results of six types of fabrics. Compare your burn results to the fabrics on the Fiber Identification Chart and identify each of the fabrics that you burned, recording your answer in the last column on your Fiber Burn Chart.

CASE CLOSED

Based on your experiment results, which suspect was wearing clothing made out of cotton and therefore is a prime suspect? Justify your answer using specific information from your burn experiment.

_____

_____

_____

_____

_____

_____

_____

_____

_____

_____

_____

_____

_____

_____

_____

_____

Fiber Burn Chart

Record your observations for each fabric swatch here.

Sample and Suspect Name	Reaction When Close to Flame	Reaction When in Flame	Color of Smoke	Odor	Identity of Fabric
A (Daniel Henry)					
B (Pat Falkenhein)					
C (Michael Daniels)					
D (Megan Steibel)					
E (Emily Hartmann)					
F (Jessica Lynn)					

Arches, Loops, and Whorls of Fun: Fingerprint Labs
Teacher Instructions

Objective:

The student will learn how to identify, dust, and lift fingerprints.

Background Research:

Fingertips are made up of friction ridges, which are raised strips of skin. These strips help us to grip things. To see how this works, try this quick demonstration. Have a friend hold a piece of paper between two fingertips. Try to pull the paper out of his grip. Notice this is very hard to do. Now have that same friend hold the paper between two knuckles or the sides of two fingers. Pull the paper now. It should easily be pulled away because the sides of our fingers do not have friction ridges. It is the impression of these ridges that we see when searching for a fingerprint.

There are three main types of fingerprint patterns: loops, whorls, and arches. Loops are found in 65% of the population, while 30% of the population has whorls, and 5% of the population has arches.

A fingerprint is identified as a loop when the ridges begin and end on the same side of the fingertip they started out on. On a whorl fingerprint, the ridges form a spiral that does not seem to begin or end on either side. The ridges in an arch print begin on one side of the fingertip and end on the opposite side, arching up in the middle like a hill.

| Whorl | Arch | Loop |

When fingerprint examiners compare two fingerprints they look for common characteristics. If the two prints have at least eight points that are the same, they can conclude that the prints match. Figure 1 includes some of the distinct characteristics they look for. Figure 2 provides an example of each characteristic as it might appear in a fingerprint.

Characteristic	Example
Fork (Bifurcation)	
Dot	
Ending Ridge	
Short Ridge	
Enclosure	

Figure 1. Fingerprint characteristic chart

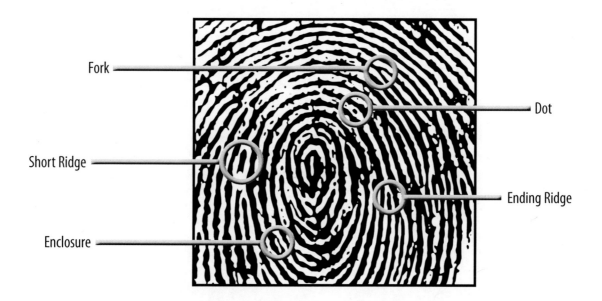

Figure 2. Fingerprint characteristics sample

The ridges on our fingers contain perspiration, oils, and amino acids, which are present on our skin. When a person touches an object, the perspiration, oils, and amino acids from the fingertips are left behind on the object. Most of the time these prints are invisible and cannot be seen by the naked eye. These types of prints are called *latent prints*. *Visible prints* are prints that can be seen. They might form because a finger comes into contact with paint, ink, or blood and then touches a surface.

To find latent prints, investigators will lightly dust a surface with a special type of powder. When the powder adheres to the oils left behind from the fingertip, the hidden fingerprint becomes visible. The powder comes in different colors, which is helpful when dealing with different colored surfaces. For example, a black powder would be used on a white surface, while a white powder would show up better on a black surface.

Depending on the type of surface the print is on, investigators might try other methods such as superglue fuming or using a chemical called *ninhydrin* to process the latent print. When superglue is heated in a sealed chamber, it forms a vapor that causes latent fingerprints to turn white. Ninhydrin reacts with the amino acids found in the oils on your skin. When a latent print is exposed to ninhydrin, it causes the print to turn reddish-purple in color.

Arches, Loops, and Whorls of Fun
Fingerprint Lab 1:
Classifying Fingerprints
Teacher Instructions

Gathering Materials:

For Lab 1 you will need magnifying glasses and highlighters or yellow markers for student use. You also will need student copies of the fingerprint lab, the Fingerprint Identification Practice Sheet, and the Fingerprints for Crime Fighting Challenge sheet on pages 44–48.

Setting Up the Lab:

1. Make copies of pages 44–48 for each student.

2. Put magnifying glasses and highlighters at your lab stations.

3. You may choose to complete this lab as a class. In this case, make magnifying glasses and highlighters available to your students at their desks.

Special Notes:

Lab 1 may be completed together as a class. The Fingerprint Identification Practice Sheet may be completed and discussed in class, and then the Crime Fighting Challenge paper may be assigned and collected for a grade.

Arches, Loops, and Whorls of Fun
Fingerprint Lab 1:
Classifying Fingerprints
Student Lab

Materials Needed:

Fingerprint Identification Practice Sheet, Crime Fighting Challenge worksheet, magnifying glass, highlighter

Essential Question:

How do fingerprint examiners identify and classify fingerprints?

Background Research:

Fingertips are made up of friction ridges, which are raised strips of skin. These strips help us to grip things. To see how this works, try this quick demonstration. Have a friend hold a piece of paper between two fingertips. Try to pull the paper out of his grip. Notice this is very hard to do. Now have that same friend hold the paper between two knuckles or the sides of two fingers. Pull the paper now. It should easily be pulled away because the sides of our fingers do not have friction ridges. It is the impression of these ridges that we see when searching for a fingerprint.

There are three main types of fingerprint patterns: loops, whorls, and arches. Loops are found in 65% of the population, while 30% of the population has whorls, and 5% of the population has arches.

A fingerprint is identified as a loop when the ridges begin and end on the same side of the fingertip they started out on. On a whorl fingerprint, the ridges form a spiral that does not seem to begin or end on either side. The ridges in an arch print begin on one side of the fingertip and end on the opposite side, arching up in the middle like a hill.

Whorl

Arch

Loop

© Prufrock Press • This page may be photocopied or reproduced with permission for classroom use only.

When fingerprint examiners compare two fingerprints they look for common characteristics. If the two prints have at least eight points that are the same, they can conclude that the prints match. Figure 1 includes some of the distinct characteristics they look for. Figure 2 provides an example of each characteristic as it might appear in a fingerprint.

Characteristic	Example
Fork (Bifurcation)	
Dot	
Ending Ridge	
Short Ridge	
Enclosure	

Figure 1. Fingerprint characteristic chart

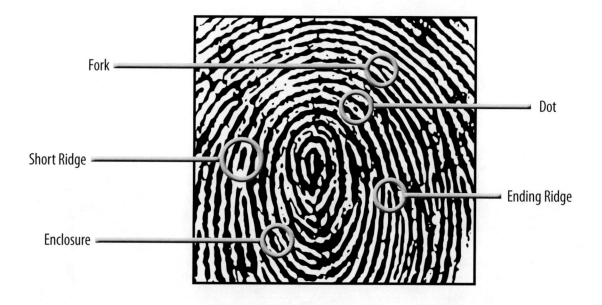

Figure 2. Fingerprint characteristics sample

The ridges on our fingers contain perspiration, oils, and amino acids, which are present on our skin. When a person touches an object, the perspiration, oils, and amino acids from the fingertips are left behind on the object. Most of the time these prints are invisible and cannot be seen by the naked eye. These types of prints are called *latent prints*. *Visible prints* are prints that can be seen. They might form because a finger comes into contact with paint, ink, or blood and then touches a surface.

To find latent prints, investigators will lightly dust a surface with a special type of powder. When the powder adheres to the oils left behind from the fingertip, the hidden fingerprint becomes visible.

Crime Fighting Challenge

Mrs. Schulz's classroom was broken into over the weekend. When she arrived at school on Monday, she discovered the glass window next to the door was broken. The police believe the thief broke the window, put his arm through the open area, and turned the knob from the inside to open the door. Police dusted the doorknob and recovered one print. Security cameras at the school identified several suspects walking through the hallway over the course of the weekend. Prints were gathered from those suspects. Carefully examine each print and compare them to the print found at the crime scene to determine whose print was left on the doorknob.

Experiment Procedures:

1. Read through the background research and look closely at the examples provided using a magnifying glass when needed.

2. Practice identifying types of fingerprints and characteristics of fingerprints by completing the Fingerprint Identification Practice Sheet. Follow the specific directions as listed on the worksheet. Be prepared to turn in this paper to your teacher if requested.

3. Look at the fingerprint samples found on the Fingerprints for Crime Fighting Challenge worksheet. Follow the directions on the paper to solve the crime fighting challenge.

CASE CLOSED Which staff member left the print on the doorknob? Describe how you know, using vocabulary such as arch, loop, whorl, fork, dot, ending ridge, and more.

_____

_____

_____

_____

_____

Fingerprint Identification Practice Sheet

1. Identify each print below as an arch, a loop, or a whorl by writing the correct name of the print on each line.

  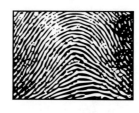

1._____ **2.**_____ **3.**_____

4._____ **5.**_____ **6.**_____

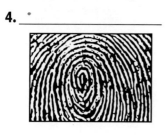 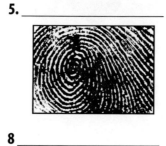 

7._____ **8**_____ **9.**_____

Fingerprint examiners identify several different characteristics when examining fingerprints. (See the Fingerprint Characteristic Chart given under background research on the lab procedures page.)

2. On the fingerprint at the bottom of the page, identify one example of each characteristic (fork, dot, ending ridge, short ridge, enclosure) by using a highlighter or yellow marker to highlight or trace over the characteristic in the print. From that characteristic, draw a line to the side of the fingerprint and then identify what the characteristic (fork, dot, enclosure, etc.) represents.

Fingerprints for Crime Fighting Challenge

Directions:

Carefully examine the print that was recovered from Mrs. Schulz's doorknob and the prints that were taken from the known suspects. Compare the prints, looking for fingerprint types such as arch, loop, whorl, and unique features such as forks, dots, and enclosures. You may need to use a magnifying glass during your examination. Determine which suspect's print matches the print left at the crime scene. Describe and justify your findings under the Cased Closed section on your lab procedures packet.

The print above was recovered from the doorknob of Mrs. Schulz's classroom door.

Prints taken from suspects:

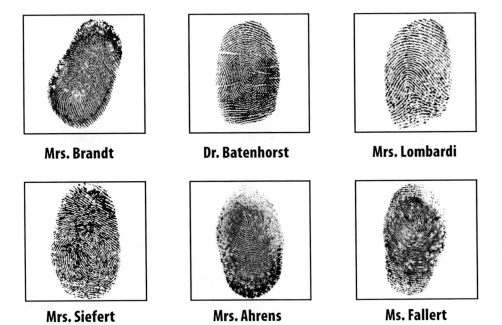

| Mrs. Brandt | Dr. Batenhorst | Mrs. Lombardi |
| Mrs. Siefert | Mrs. Ahrens | Ms. Fallert |

Arches, Loops, and Whorls of Fun
Fingerprint Lab 1 Extension:
Balloon Prints
Teacher Instructions

Objective:

The student will be able to identify his own fingerprint pattern as an arch, a loop, or a whorl.

Gathering Materials:

The student will be placing an inked finger on a balloon and enlarging it to better see the print pattern. You will need white or light-colored balloons (approximate size 10 inches), one for each student. You also will need a black stamp pad. This is a large-group activity led by the teacher so no student lab pages are needed.

Setting Up and Completing the Experiment:

1. On the chalkboard write the headings *arch*, *loop*, and *whorl*.

2. Before handing out the deflated balloons to students, demonstrate Steps 3–6.

3. Inflate the balloon so that the balloon has just begun to fill up. Do not overinflate the balloon. It should be barely inflated.

4. While holding the partially inflated balloon closed with your left hand, press the tip of your right pointer finger onto a black inkpad.

5. Slowly, carefully, and firmly press the inked finger onto the middle or the widest part of the slightly inflated balloon. A small print will be left behind.

6. Now, continue blowing up the balloon to a normal inflated size. As you inflate the balloon, the fingerprint will enlarge allowing you to easily see the type of fingerprint you have without the use of a magnifying glass.

7. After demonstrating the procedure, have students ink and stamp their right pointer finger on their balloons. Ask them to identify the print as an arch, loop, or whorl.

8. After each child has identified his or her print, survey the class and keep a tally of the number of students who have loops, arches, and whorls on the right pointer finger. Record this information on the chart on the board. Does the majority of the class have loops? Remember 60% of the population has loop patterns, while 35% of the population has whorls, and 5% has arches. How does your classroom compare to these statistics?

Special Notes:

This is a really great way for students to see the type (arch, loop, whorl) of fingerprint they have without the use of a magnifying glass. Students love this activity!

Hint:

Tell students not to tie their balloons in a knot. When they are done looking at the print they can deflate the balloon and take it home to show their parents. It can be difficult to continue teaching the class with inflated balloons floating around the room, which is another great reason for not tying the balloon. Here are other thoughts for students to pursue: Is the print pattern the same for every finger on a person? Do print patterns run in a family? Ask students to print members of their family to see if there is a similarity in patterns.

Arches, Loops, and Whorls of Fun
Fingerprint Lab 2:
Dusting and Lifting Prints
Teacher Instructions

Gathering Materials:

For Lab 2 you will need some sort of ceramic tile for students to place their fingerprints on. A smooth, white tile works the best. If you don't have a tile, you can always use the surface of a desktop. You will need fingerprint dusting powder, which can be purchased from a variety of companies (see Reference Materials on pp. 136–137). I recommend purchasing magnetic powder, which is much easier and cleaner to work with. A magnetic wand is needed to apply the powder. In addition, you will need newspapers to cover your work area (unless you are dusting on the desktop), clear tape wide enough to cover a fingerprint, and one note card per student. Paper towels and water should be available to clean the tile. You will also need copies of the Dusting and Lifting Prints student lab on pages 53–55.

Setting Up the Lab:

1. Make copies of pages 53–55 for each student.

2. Place newspaper down on the table or desk before placing the tile on top of the newspaper.

3. If you are using a large area such as a desktop or table, section off a smaller area with masking tape. This will give the students a smaller area to place their fingerprint, and therefore a smaller area to dust. This will save on powder and make clean up easier. If you are using a large tile, you also may want to designate a smaller area on the tile for students to work with.

4. Place the tile, magnetic powder, and wand at the station.

5. Have paper towels and a squirt bottle with water available for students to use to clean the tile when they have finished.

6. Before allowing students to complete the lab, demonstrate how to use the magnetic powder and wand, emphasizing the fact that very little powder is actually needed to dust for the print. You also may want to show how to place the tape on a print and how to remove it.

Special Notes:

Steps 3–6 in the student experiment procedures are written for using magnetic powder. If you use nonmagnetic powder, you may need to alter these steps slightly.

Be sure to try dusting on the chosen tile or surface before conducting the experiment with the class. Some tiles are easier to lift prints from than others.

I purchased a 1-ounce jar of black magnetic powder and a wand from a company called Kinderprint (see Reference Materials). Both products were affordably priced. You may want to purchase two 1-ounce jars and two wands so you can set up multiple stations.

Arches, Loops, and Whorls of Fun Fingerprint Lab 2: Dusting and Lifting Prints
Student Lab

Materials Needed:

Ceramic tile, magnetic fingerprint dust and wand, newspapers, clear tape, note cards

Essential Question:

How do crime scene technicians locate and lift a print from an object?

Background Research:

We learned in the first fingerprint lab that fingertips are made up of friction ridges, which are raised strips of skin. These ridges on our fingers contain perspiration, oils, and amino acids, which are present on our skin. When a person touches an object, the perspiration, oils, and amino acids from the fingertips are left behind on the object. Most of the time these prints are invisible and cannot be seen by the naked eye. These types of prints are called *latent prints*. *Visible prints* are prints that can be seen. They might form because a finger comes into contact with paint, ink, or blood and then touches a surface.

To find latent prints, investigators will lightly dust a surface with a special type of powder. When the powder adheres to the oils left behind from the fingertip, the hidden fingerprint becomes visible. The powder comes in different colors, which is helpful when dealing with different colored surfaces. For example, a black powder would be used on a white surface, while a white powder would show up better on a black surface.

Depending on the type of surface the print is on, investigators might try other methods such as superglue fuming or using a chemical called *ninhydrin* to process the latent print. When superglue is heated in a sealed chamber, it forms a vapor that causes latent fingerprints to turn white. Ninhydrin reacts with the amino acids found in the oils on your skin. When a latent print is exposed to ninhydrin, it causes the print to turn reddish-purple in color.

Crime Fighting Challenge

You are a part of a crime scene investigative team. Your job is to discover and lift a fingerprint left behind at a crime scene. Follow the procedures below to complete this challenge.

Name:_____ **Date:**_____

1. Complete this experiment with a partner. Determine who will be Student 1 and who will be Student 2.

2. Student 1 should close his eyes or walk away from the work area. Student 2 will run his fingers through his hair or over his skin to pick up oil on his fingertip. Carefully place one fingertip on the tile so that your fingerprint is left behind. Do not tell your partner where you placed the fingerprint. Student 1 should follow Steps 3–8 to locate and recover Student 2's hidden fingerprint.

3. Carefully open the jar of black magnetic dust. Note: This powder is really messy so take great care not to spill it.

4. Pick up the magnetic wand, which is used in dusting the print. Make sure the plunger of the wand is pushed (gently) into the casing of the wand. Dip the wand lightly into the jar of dust. You don't need to bury the wand, just touch the surface of the magnetic powder. When you pull the wand out of the jar, you should see the magnetic dust hanging from the bottom of the wand. Use the powder sparingly, you don't need a lot.

5. Lightly run the wand over the surface of the tile. Do not push down hard on the wand. Use a twirling motion, just barely touching the tile. Stop when you can see the outline of the fingerprint.

6. Move the wand back to the open jar. Pull the plunger out to release the magnetic hold. The remaining magnetic powder should fall back into the jar.

7. Tear off a piece of clear tape a little larger than the fingerprint. Hold the tape by the very ends to avoid putting your fingerprints on the tape while holding it. Place the tape over the exposed fingerprint on the tile. Press the tape firmly over the print, being careful not to create air bubbles in the tape. When you have the tape pressed over the print, you may need to lightly run your finger over the tape, pressing down gently to ensure that the magnetic powder left on the print sticks to the tape. Slowly peel the tape off of the tile.

8. Place the tape with the lifted print on to the note card provided. Carefully clean off the tile.

9. Repeat Steps 2–8 so that Student 1 is placing his print and Student 2 dusts and recovers the print. Show your teacher your recovered prints. Be prepared to turn in the note cards containing your prints.

CASE CLOSED

Answer these questions in sentences to show you have mastered the art of fingerprint recovery.

1. After touching the tile with your finger, a print, although invisible, was left behind. Explain why this happens.

_____

_____

_____

2. Why does a latent (invisible) fingerprint become visible after dusting it with powder?

_____

_____

_____

3. Although you did not wear gloves while dusting for and lifting the print from the tile, it is required for technicians working a crime scene. Why must they wear gloves while processing evidence such as fingerprints?

_____

_____

_____

4. What, in your opinion, is the most difficult part of lifting fingerprints to be used as evidence? Be detailed in your answer.

_____

_____

_____

Arches, Loops, and Whorls of Fun
Fingerprint Lab 2 Extension 1:
Processing Prints Using Ninhydrin
Teacher Instructions

Objective:

The student will be able to recover a latent print from paper using a chemical process involving ninhydrin.

Additional Background Research:

Ninhydrin is a chemical used to detect amino acids found in the oils on our skin. When fingerprints are left on paper, ninhydrin is the best method to use for recovery. Unlike using powder, ninhydrin stains the prints on the paper a purple color, which allows the prints to remain indefinitely. It is not possible to lift and preserve a print found on paper by dusting it with powder.

Gathering Materials:

This lab uses ninhydrin, which can be purchased at an affordable price from a science supply company (see Reference Materials on pp. 136–137). The ninhydrin will be poured into a disposable pie tin. A paper with latent prints is needed, as is a pair of tweezers or tongs to hold the paper. An iron may be used to speed up the chemical reaction. Newspapers may be placed on the tabletop to protect the surface. This is a large-group demonstration led by the teacher so no student lab pages are needed.

Setting Up and Completing the Experiment:

1. Begin by passing around a small piece of paper and have students touch it with their fingers.

2. Pour a small amount of ninhydrin into a disposable tin pie pan.

3. Using tweezers, submerge the paper in the ninhydrin. Let it soak long enough for the paper to be saturated and then remove it.

4. Place the wet paper on newspaper to allow it to dry. Although it may take a while, the latent fingerprints will turn up reddish-purple.

5. To speed up this chemical reaction, run a hot iron over the paper after removing it from the ninhydrin. The heat from the iron will accelerate the process and the prints should become visible immediately.

6. The darkness of the prints will depend on the amount of amino acids found in the person's skin.

Special Notes:

Take necessary safety precautions when working with a chemical. Ninhydrin has a strong odor, so it is best used in a well-ventilated area.

You may choose to have students complete this lab at an independent station or have each child give you his own sheet of paper with just his prints on it.

Arches, Loops, and Whorls of Fun
Fingerprint Lab 2 Extension 2:
Processing Prints Using Superglue Fuming
Teacher Instructions

Objective:

The student will be able to recover a latent print from a surface using superglue fuming.

Gathering Materials:

You will need a tube of superglue, a "boat" made out of tinfoil, a soda can containing latent prints, a small aquarium or box, and a hot plate or mug warmer.

Setting Up and Completing the Lab:

1. You will need to create some type of airtight chamber. You can use a small aquarium and fashion a lid out of foil or even use a small box. If you use a box you will need to tape over any holes in the box.

2. Place a hot plate into the chamber.

3. Make a "boat" out of tinfoil and drop superglue, about the size of a nickel, on the foil. Place this on the hot plate.

4. Put an empty soda can that has been handled (and thus contains latent prints) into the chamber.

5. Seal the chamber, making it airtight. Plug in the hot plate.

6. Latent fingerprints on the soda can will turn white and should show up within 15 minutes.

Special Notes:

Take great care when removing the lid to avoid breathing in superglue fumes. You may want to try a variety of objects to see how the fuming works on different materials.

After completing all fingerprint labs, ask the students to predict which method (dusting, ninhydrin, superglue fuming) would work best on a variety of surfaces such as glass, cardboard, and plastic.

All Cracked Up: Glass Fracture Lab
Teacher Instructions

Objective:

The student will learn how investigators use glass fracture patterns to determine the order in which bullet holes were made.

Background Research:

Gunshots in glass can play a vital role in a crime scene investigation. With multiple gunshot markings, police can determine which shot was fired first, then second, and so on. It also is possible to determine the direction from which the gun was fired. This lab will address the topic of the order in which bullets were fired at a crime scene.

When a bullet passes through a window, it breaks the glass in two ways: radially (lines) and concentrically (circles). A radial fracture is a line/crack that starts from the point where the bullet hit the window (point of impact) and extends out. A concentric crack creates "circles" of broken glass around the bullet entrance point.

When a bullet hits a window, the glass bends as far as possible and then it breaks. The resulting hole often resembles a "crater" and is bordered by concentric and radial cracks. Because the entrance hole is always smaller than the exit hole, investigators can determine if the gun was fired from the inside or the outside of the window.

More than one bullet may pass through the same window. By looking at the fracture lines it is possible to determine the order in which the bullets hit the window. A fracture line cannot pass through an existing fracture line. So, the fracture lines coming after the first one will be stopped. Look at Figure 1 below.

Follow the fracture lines from point A. They are not "stopped" by any other lines. Bullet A was the first bullet through the window. Follow the lines from point B. The fractures from B are stopped by the fractures from bullet A but not by the fractures from bullet C. Bullet B was the second shot fired. Notice that the fractures from bullet C are stopped by the fractures from both A and B, so C was the last shot fired.

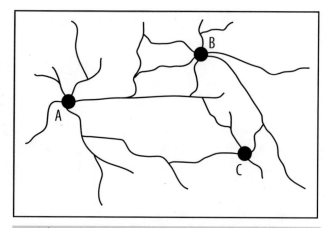

Figure 1. Glass cracked from gunshot.

Gathering Materials:

You will need a window. If you have windows in your classroom, you may use one of those windows or you may choose to use a free standing window. Check with a remodeling company or a company that replaces windows and ask for an old window to keep in your classroom. A marker is needed for drawing the fracture lines on the glass. You also will need student copies of the Glass Fracture Lab on pages 61–62.

Setting Up the Lab:

1. Make copies of the All Cracked Up Student Lab on pages 61–62.

2. Use a transparency marker to create lines or cracks on the window. If you are using a window that is free standing you may want to use a permanent marker.

3. Label three different points on the window with A, B, and C.

4. Point B should be the first shot fired, so draw the lines from point B first. Some lines may be long while others are short in length. The lines from point B should not be stopped by or run into any other lines. Next, draw lines from point A and have some of them run into the lines from point B. Finally, draw lines from point C. The lines coming from point C should run into or be stopped by the lines from both points B and A.

5. Place materials at the glass fracture station.

Special Notes:

This lab is understood easily by most students and doesn't take long to complete. Although the lab focuses on determining the order in which the bullets were fired, some information on how police can determine whether a bullet was fired from inside or outside of the window also is included. If you don't have access to a window, you also could use the glass from a picture frame.

Name:_____ Date:_____

All Cracked Up: Glass Fracture Lab
Student Lab

Materials Needed:

Window (or glass) with simulated shots

Essential Question:

How can you determine which bullet hole, out of several bullet holes, was fired through the window first?

Background Research:

Gunshots in glass can play a vital role in a crime scene investigation. With multiple gunshot markings, police can determine which shot was fired first, then second, and so on. It also is possible to determine the direction from which the gun was fired. This lab will address the topic of the order in which bullets were fired at a crime scene.

When a bullet passes through a window, it breaks the glass in two ways: radially (lines) and concentrically (circles). A radial fracture is a line/crack that starts from the point where the bullet hit the window (point of impact) and extends out. A concentric crack creates "circles" of broken glass around the bullet entrance point.

When a bullet hits a window, the glass bends as far as possible and then it breaks. The resulting hole often resembles a "crater" and is bordered by concentric and radial cracks. Because the entrance hole is always smaller than the exit hole, investigators can determine if the gun was fired from the inside or the outside of the window.

More than one bullet may pass through the same window. By looking at the fracture lines it is possible to determine the order in which the bullets hit the window. A fracture line cannot pass through an existing fracture line. So, the fracture lines coming after the first one will be stopped. Look at the example on this page.

Follow the fracture lines from point A. They are not "stopped" by any other lines. Bullet A was the first bullet through the window. Follow the lines from point B. The fractures from B are stopped by the fractures from bullet A but not by the fractures from bullet C. Bullet B was the second shot fired. Notice that the fractures from bullet C are stopped by the fractures from both A and B, so C was the last shot fired.

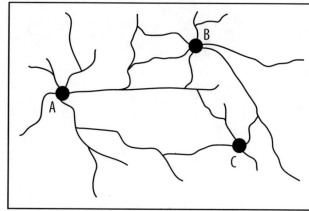

Example of glass cracked by a gunshot.

At 2:52 a.m. neighbors reported hearing a disturbance at 1717 Herring Way. When police arrived, they tried to gain access to the house. The owner of the home, Stan Stumpey, refused to let them in. Officer Johnson went around to the back of the house and, looking through the kitchen window, identified the armed suspect. Three gunshots were fired through a kitchen window and Stan was injured. After requesting medical help for Stan, police examined the kitchen and saw three bullet holes in the kitchen window.

Officer Johnson claims that while she was outside, Stan fired his gun and that she, Officer Johnson, fired her gun twice only after Stan first fired at her. Stan claims he was firing in self-defense and fired his gun once only after the officer shot the first two bullets. Ballistic experts identified the bullet hole marked as B as coming from the inside of the house, thus being fired from Stan's gun. The bullet holes marked A and C were identified as coming from the outside of the house, which would mean they were fired from Officer Johnson's gun. Follow the experiment procedures to determine who fired the first shot.

Experiment Procedures:

Carefully examine the glass window, taking care not to touch the glass and destroy valuable evidence. Based on your observations, answer the following questions:

1. Which bullet was fired first? A, B, or C? Explain how you know.

_____

_____

2. Which bullet was fired last? A, B, or C? Explain how you know.

_____

_____

CASE CLOSED

Based on your examination of the window and the fracture lines from the bullet holes, who fired the first shot, Officer Johnson or Stan? Explain, in detail, how you reached your conclusion.

_____

_____

_____

_____

_____

Dot Your I's and Cross Your T's: Handwriting Characteristics Lab

Teacher Instructions

Objective:

The student will learn the 12 characteristics handwriting experts use when analyzing handwriting and the student will apply the characteristics in examining a sample of his own handwriting.

Background Research:

When we first learn how to write, we are taught to form letters by copying examples in a rote way so that at a young age our handwriting looks a lot like everyone else's. As we get older we start developing our own unique writing styles. Our writing becomes subconscious, so that we don't even think about how we form letters. Some people mix cursive with print writing. Some people embellish their writing with fancy swirls. Some write letters in a word close together while others spread them apart. Some slant their letters to the right, while others slant their letters to the left.

It is the combination of these factors that make a person's handwriting unique. Experts are able to examine these unique characteristics and compare a known handwriting sample to a questioned sample and determine if the same person scripted both samples. Experts look for 12 basic characteristics when comparing handwriting samples. See the Basic Characteristics for Analyzing Handwriting Reference Pages (see pp. 66–68) for a description of these characteristics.

Gathering Materials:

You will need student copies of the lab on pages 64–70 and magnifying glasses.

Setting Up the Lab:

1. Make copies of the Dot Your I's and Cross Your T's Student Lab and the Basic Characteristics for Analyzing Handwriting handout on pages 64–70.

2. Place magnifying glasses and the student lab papers at the handwriting characteristics station.

Special Notes:

You may want to discuss with students your expectations for the official report paragraph for the crime fighting challenge.

Dot Your 'I's and Cross Your 'T's: Handwriting Characteristics Lab
Student Lab

Materials Needed:

Blue or black pen, Basic Characteristics for Analyzing Handwriting Reference Page, Handwriting Self-Analysis Page, one sheet of lined notebook paper, a magnifying glass (optional)

Essential Question:

What characteristics make a person's handwriting unique?

Background Research:

When we first learn how to write, we are taught to form letters by copying examples in a rote way so that at a young age our handwriting looks a lot like everyone else's. As we get older we start developing our own unique writing styles. Our writing becomes subconscious, so that we don't even think about how we form letters. Some people mix cursive with print writing. Some people embellish their writing with fancy swirls. Some write letters in a word close together while others spread them apart. Some slant their letters to the right, while others slant their letters to the left.

It is the combination of these factors that make a person's handwriting unique. Experts are able to examine these unique characteristics and compare a known handwriting sample to a questioned sample and determine if the same person scripted both samples. Experts look for 12 basic characteristics when comparing handwriting samples. See the Basic Characteristics for Analyzing Handwriting Reference Page for a description of these characteristics.

Crime Fighting Challenge

You are applying for a job as a handwriting expert for the FBI. As part of the application process, you must submit an example of your work. Follow the experiment procedures to analyze your own handwriting sample and then summarize your findings.

Experiment Procedures:

1. Write the paragraph on the following page in cursive on a sheet of lined notebook paper. Write in your normal style.

At 4:52 a.m., police officers responded to reports of a bank robbery at First Bank and Trust. Upon arriving at the scene, they discovered a window that was broken by an unknown object. Inside the bank they found footprints leading to the bank's vault. Upon further inspection, it was determined the footprints were made by two separate individuals. The investigation continued as detectives processed the crime scene, recovering additional pieces of vital evidence.

2. Carefully examine the paragraph you just wrote using a magnifying glass when necessary.

3. Refer back to the Basic Characteristics for Analyzing Handwriting Reference Page and analyze your handwriting for each type of characteristic. Record your observations on the Handwriting: Self-Analysis page.

4. When you are finished, compare your handwriting sample to a classmate's handwriting sample. Discuss the characteristics that make each of your handwriting unique.

CASE CLOSED

Write a detailed, descriptive paragraph in which you summarize the overall characteristics of your handwriting sample. Be sure to include terms such as line spacing, connecting strokes, and unusual letter formation. Your paragraph should be written as if it was an official FBI report. You may choose to start your paragraph in this way, "The questioned document I examined contained many unique characteristics . . ."

_____
_____
_____
_____
_____
_____
_____
_____
_____
_____
_____

Basic Characteristics
for Analyzing Handwriting
Reference Page

Handwriting experts usually look for the following 12 characteristics when examining handwriting samples.

1. Line quality: Are the lines smooth or shaky?

Smooth writing

Solving crimes is a challenging job.

Shaky writing

Solving crimes is a challenging job.

2. Spacing of words and letters: Are the words and letters close together or far apart?

Words written close together

Solving crimes is a challenging job.

Words written further apart

Solving crimes is a challenging job.

3. Ratio of relative height, width, and size of letters: Do they vary or stay the same?

Text starts small and then gets larger

Solving crimes is a challenging job.

4. Pen lifts and separations: How are new letters or words formed? Is the pen lifted and started again?

Letters connected between words or pen strokes left on paper between words

Solving crimes is a challenging job.

Definite pen break between words

Solving crimes is a challenging job.

5. Connecting strokes: How are capital letters connected to lowercase letters?

Capital letters connected to the lower case letter that follows

> *Detective Will E. Catchem is a Crime Scene Investigator.*

Capital letters not connected to the lower case letter that follows

> *Detective Will E. Catchem is a Crime Scene Investigator.*

6. Beginning and ending strokes: How do words or letters begin or end?

Letters end with a flourish

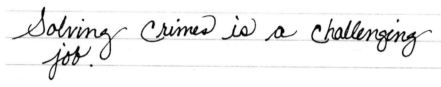

Letters end abruptly

> *Solving crimes is a challenging job.*

7. Unusual letter formation: Are any letters written with a tail? Is cursive and printed writing used in combination?

Letters with "tails" (g, j, p) circle back up and others end with a curl

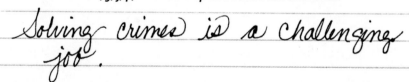

Letters with "tails" go straight down and end and others have no curl. Cursive is mixed with print

> *Solving crimes is a challenging job.*

8. Shading or pen pressure: Are letters written unusually dark or light?

Light print

Solving crimes is a challenging job.

Dark print

Solving crimes is a challenging job.

9. Slant of letters: Does the writing slant forward, backward, or remain straight up?

Right slant

Solving crimes is a challenging job.

Left slant

Solving crimes is a challenging job.

10. Baseline habits: Is the writing above or below a line?

Letters above or not touching the line

Solving crimes is a challenging job.

Letters touching or below the line

Solving crimes is a challenging job.

11. Flourishes or embellishments: Are there extras like hearts to dot an "i" or loops added to letters?

Extra loops or curls or dots

Solving crimes is a challenging job.

12. Placement of diacritics: Are the "t's" crossed distinctly or "i's" dotted to the right or left of the letter?

T's are crossed with an upward slant, I's dotted with a upward "dash"

Detective Will E. Catchem is a Crime Scene Investigator.

Name:_____ Date:_____

Handwriting: Self-Analysis

Carefully examine the handwriting sample that you produced in Step 1 of the experiment procedures. Analyze and describe the unique characteristics in your handwriting sample, recording the information in the table on the next page. Give at least one example of a word that the characteristic appeared in.

Look at the example analysis of two handwriting characteristics in the table below.

Table 1	
Handwriting Characteristic	**Description of How It Appears in Your Sample**
Connecting strokes	Capital letters are never connected to the next letter in the word. For example, in the words "First," "Bank," and "Trust," the F, B, and T are not connected to the letter that follows.
Unusual letter formation	Every time a lower case "g" is written in the sample ("arriving," "leading," "recovering"), the tail of the "g" is drawn down as a straight line. It is not curved.

Name:_____ Date:_____

Table 2

Handwriting Characteristic	Description of How It Appears in Your Sample
1. Line quality	
2. Spacing of words and letters	
3. Ratio of relative height, width, and size of letters	
4. Pen lifts and separations	
5. Connecting strokes	
6. Beginning and end strokes	
7. Unusual letter formation	
8. Shading or pen pressure	
9. Slant of letters	
10. Baseline habits	
11. Flourishes or embellishments	
12. Placement of diacritics	

The Genuine Article: Handwriting Forgery Lab
Teacher Instructions

Objective:

The student will analyze signatures and determine which ones have been forged.

Background Research:

Signing another person's name is the most common type of forgery. There are three ways a person may forge a name. A *traced forgery* is done when a real signature is traced onto a different document. In a *simulated forgery*, the forger carefully writes the name freehand by looking at the real signature. The forger often will practice writing the name repeatedly until he is able to write it without hesitation. The last type of forgery is known as a *blind forgery*. In this type of forgery, the forger uses his own handwriting to sign someone else's name. He makes no effort to disguise his handwriting and may not even know what the genuine signature looks like. No matter what type of forgery is used, experts still refer back to the 12 basic handwriting characteristics to examine the forged signature.

Gathering Materials:

You will need student copies of The Genuine Article Student Lab on pages 72–75, magnifying glasses, black ink pens, and scissors.

Setting Up the Lab:

1. Make copies of the student lab on pages 72–75.

2. Place the magnifying glasses and the student lab papers at the appropriate station.

Special Notes:

Student partners should use the same pen when writing their signatures in the sample boxes. Using different pens with varying thickness or color may sway the examiner's opinion when analyzing the signatures.

The Genuine Article: Handwriting Forgery
Student Lab

Materials Needed:

Black ink pen, Signature Samples page, magnifying glass (optional), scissors

Essential Question:

How can you determine if a signature has been forged?

Background Research:

Signing another person's name is the most common type of forgery. There are three ways a person may forge a name. A *traced forgery* is done when a real signature is traced onto a different document. In a *simulated forgery*, the forger carefully writes the name freehand by looking at the real signature. The forger often will practice writing the name repeatedly until he is able to write it without hesitation. The last type of forgery is known as a *blind forgery*. In this type of forgery, the forger uses his own handwriting to sign someone else's name. He makes no effort to disguise his handwriting and may not even know what the genuine signature looks like. No matter what type of forgery is used, experts still refer back to the 12 basic handwriting characteristics to examine the forged signature.

Crime Fighting Challenge

You are a handwriting expert who has been asked to examine two sets of handwritten signatures. With each genuine signature sample you will have three questionable samples to analyze. Compare these three questionable samples to the genuine signature. Determine which two samples out of the three have been forged. Identify the sample that was written by the same person who wrote the genuine sample. Repeat your examination using the second set of signatures.

Experiment Procedures:

Part 1. Preparing the signatures.

1. You will be working with a partner for this lab. Determine who will be Student A and who will be Student B.

2. Cut apart the boxes on the Signature Sample page.

3. Using a black pen, Student A should write his name in cursive in the box marked "Genuine Signature A."

4. Student A should choose one additional box (either signature box A1, A2, or A3) and write his name in that box.

5. Student B will try to copy the signature in two different ways. First, student B will trace over the signature by placing one of the remaining signature boxes (containing the letter A) on top of the paper containing the genuine signature A in it.

6. After tracing the name the first time, student B will try to write the signature again in the last available signature box marked A. This time the student will just look at the signature and try to duplicate it freehand. No tracing allowed.

7. Repeat the procedures again. This time Student B will write her name in cursive in the box marked "Genuine Signature B." Student B will choose another box (B1, B2, or B3) and write her signature again.

8. Student A will now try to copy the signature by tracing over the name in one box and by copying it freehand in the last remaining box.

9. Clip the boxes representing Student A's signature together and do the same for Student B's signature boxes.

10. Let your teacher know that you are finished. Your teacher will direct you to another group of students.

Part 2. Analyzing the signatures.

1. Your teacher has assigned you and your partner another group to switch signature cards with. Give that group both sets of signature cards and in return take both of their sets of signature cards.

2. Look at the sets of cards marked A, A1, A2, and A3. Examine the genuine signature carefully. Now look at the signatures on the three remaining cards. Identify which of the three (A1, A2, or A3) matches the genuine signature card and therefore was written by the same student as A. Record your responses under "Case Closed."

3. Repeat this procedure with the cards marked B, B1, B2, and B3.

4. After you have finished your analysis, check with the students in the group who gave you the cards to see if you correctly identified the signature.

CASE CLOSED

1. Which card (A1, A2, or A3) matched card A? Describe how you determined your answer, referring back to the basic characteristics of handwriting and using vocabulary such as slant of letters, baseline habits, connecting strokes, and more.

_____

_____

_____

_____

_____

_____

_____

2. Which card (B1, B2, or B3) matched card B? Describe how you determined your answer, referring back to the basic characteristics of handwriting and using vocabulary such as slant of letters, baseline habits, connecting strokes, and more.

_____

_____

_____

_____

_____

_____

_____

Signature Samples

Cut the boxes apart before writing on them.

Genuine Signature A

Signature A1

Signature A2

Signature A3

Genuine Signature B

Signature B1

Signature B2

Signature B3

Grades Gone Goofy: Altered Grades Lab
Teacher Instructions

Objective:
The student will analyze a handwritten document to determine if the document has been altered.

Background Research:
Document examiners often are called on to analyze handwritten documents to check for forgeries or altered documents. Similar to a fingerprint, each person has a unique style of writing. By studying these unique characteristics in writing, document examiners are able to determine if the same person wrote two separate documents. Document examiners also will evaluate the type of ink used on a document. If more than one type of ink is present, it might suggest the document was altered at a later date.

Gathering Materials:
You will need a blank page from a grade book or some other type of grid for recording student grades. You also will need a magnifying glass and student copies of the Grades Gone Goofy Student Lab on pages 78–80.

Setting Up the Lab:
1. Make copies of the student lab on pages 78–80.

2. Write the following names and grades onto a grade book page or grid.

Student name	Research HW (30 pts.)	Outline HW (100 pts.)	Forensics Test (100 pts.)
Bennett, Kailey	30	98	75
Carrie, Megan	28	88	96
Gregory, Ty	28	60	85
Iversen, Angie	20	84	75
Katharine, Karin	30	97	90
Kelly, John	30	88	92
Krueger, Cindy	27	95	92
Marron, Jim	11	78	75
McAllister, Flash	30	45	95
Neal, Janel	30	93	97
O'Neill, Brooke	20	10	84
Roessler, Holly	15	98	98
Ronald, Nicholas	30	98	85
Stevens, Noah	28	76	39

3. Using a slightly different shade of ink, alter the following scores:

Angie Iversen: change the 20 to a 30 and the 75 to a 95.

Jim Marron: change the 11 to 24, and the 75 to a 95.

Flash McAllister: change the 45 to a 95.

Brooke O'Neill: change the 10 to a 100.

Noah Stevens: change the 39 to an 89.

Special Notes:

When altering the grades be sure to use a different shade of ink. You also might want to make the altered numbers slightly different. For example, when you alter the three to make it an eight, draw the eight so it looks like two equal-sized circles on top of each other. The nonaltered eights in your grade book could be drawn differently so that perhaps the loop on the top of the eight is bigger than the loop on the bottom. You do not need to make a grade sheet for every student to examine. Make enough grade sheets to cover your lab stations.

Grades Gone Goofy: Altered Grades Lab
Student Lab

Materials Needed:

Grade book sheet, magnifying glass, Grade Sheet Analysis Chart

Essential Question:

How can you, by examining handwriting and ink, determine if a grade was altered in a grade book?

Background Research:

Document examiners often are called on to analyze handwritten documents to check for forgeries or altered documents. Similar to a fingerprint, each person has a unique style of writing. By studying these unique characteristics in writing, document examiners are able to determine if the same person wrote two separate documents. Document examiners also will evaluate the type of ink used on a document. If more than one type of ink is present, it might suggest the document was altered at a later date.

Crime Fighting Challenge

History teacher Mr. Smith was preparing student grades for third quarter reports. He took the grades that were recorded in his grade book and entered them into his computerized grade book program. When the accumulated scores were averaged, he was surprised to see that several students that he expected to be doing poorly actually were doing quite well. On closer examination of his grade book, it appears that several grades may have been altered. Follow the experiment procedures to identify the altered grades.

Experiment Procedures:

1. Using a magnifying glass, examine the teacher grade book sheet. Carefully inspect each student's grade entry taking great care not to compromise the evidence by marking on it in any way. In particular, look for varying shades of ink or unique formation of numbers.

2. List and describe any suspicious marks you see. Use the Grade Sheet Analysis Chart to organize and record your findings. In the column titled, "Original Score," write what you believe to be the score that was originally entered in the grade book. *Note:* You may not need all of the rows.

CASE CLOSED

After completing your examination of the evidence and filling in the chart, summarize your findings by writing which student(s) had altered scores on which assignment(s). Make sure the evidence to support your claims is entered in the Grade Sheet Analysis Chart.

_____

_____

_____

_____

_____

_____

_____

_____

_____

_____

_____

_____

_____

_____

_____

_____

_____

Grade Sheet Analysis Chart

Name: _____   Date: _____

Carefully examine the grade book paper. Record your observations here.

Student Name	Assignment	Original Score	Altered Score	What Do You See That Makes You Suspect It Was Altered?

The Type to Commit a Crime:
Typewritten Documents Lab
Teacher Instructions

Objective:

The student will learn how to examine typewritten documents and identify matching print types.

Background Research:

A document examiner analyzes written documents. He may study handwriting, typewriting, paper, ink, and any other features of documents. Although computers are much more commonly used today than typewriters, document examiners still may be required to analyze text from a typewriter. Types come in a variety of sizes and styles and as typewriters become old and worn, they may begin to make unique marks when printing. The FBI keeps a file of the makes and models of typewriters and may compare the type in a document to the known existing typewriters to identify the possible source of the typed document.

Gathering Materials:

You will need student copies of The Type to Commit a Crime Student Lab on pages 82–84 and magnifying glasses.

Setting Up the Lab:

1. Make copies of the student lab on pages 82–84.

2. Place magnifying glasses and the student lab papers at the typewritten documents station.

Special Notes:

Monitor students during the lab to make sure they are both sketching and describing in words the unique characteristics of the various letters.

The Type to Commit a Crime: Typewritten Documents Lab
Student Lab

Materials Needed:

Suspect Sample Documents worksheet, magnifying glass

Essential Question:

How can unique printing characteristics be used to identify and match typewritten documents?

Background Research:

A document examiner analyzes written documents. He may study handwriting, typewriting, paper, ink, and any other features of documents. Although computers are much more commonly used today than typewriters, document examiners still may be required to analyze text from a typewriter. Types come in a variety of sizes and styles and as typewriters become old and worn, they may begin to make unique marks when printing. The FBI keeps a file of the makes and models of typewriters and may compare the type in a document to the known existing typewriters to identify the possible source of the typed document.

Crime Fighting Challenge

Last month the Brown Bank and Trust was robbed. A person in a ski mask handed the teller this typewritten note:

> This is a hold up. Give me all of your cash. Don't call the police. Follow my directions and you won't get hurt.

Document examiners have determined that the note was typed using a typewriter. Police have several suspects who happen to own typewriters. Your challenge is to examine the type print on the note given to the bank teller and to examine the prints made from the typewriters of the suspects to determine who typed the note and likely robbed the bank.

Experiment Procedures:

Carefully examine the note given to the teller in the bank robbery using a magnifying glass. Pay special attention to the spacing between letters and words, and any unique formations of letters such as the use of straight lines versus curved lines. Then, examine the samples taken from the typewriters found in the suspects' houses. Answer the following questions on a separate sheet of paper or in your lab notebooks.

1. How does the "h" in the robbery note compare to the "h" from Christopher's sample? How does it compare to the "h" in Diana's sample? (For both samples, sketch and then describe using words.)

2. How does the "a" in the robbery note compare to the "a" from Olivia's sample? How does it compare to the "a" in Karen's sample? (For both samples, sketch and then describe using words.)

3. How does the "m" in the robbery note compare to the "m" from Savannah's sample? How does it compare to the "m" in Ashley's sample? (For both samples, sketch and then describe using words.)

4. How does the "y" in the robbery note compare to the "y" from Steven's sample? How does it compare to the "y" in Glenn's sample? (For both samples, sketch and then describe using words.)

5. Examine the apostrophe found in the robbery note. Compare this to all nine of the suspect samples. Based on the formation of the apostrophe, which samples can you rule out? In other words, which samples are definitely not a match based on this characteristic? Explain your answer.

6. Examine the capital "T" found in the robbery note. Compare this to all nine of the suspect samples. Based on the formation of the "T," which samples can you rule out? Explain your answer.

CASE CLOSED

Based on your analysis and observations, which suspect owned the typewriter that matched the note used in the bank robbery? Explain how you arrived at your answer, using specific characteristics of the letters as supporting details.

_____

_____

_____

_____

_____

The Type to Commit a Crime: Typewritten Documents Lab
Suspect Sample Documents

The samples below were taken from typewriters found at each suspect's house: The samples are identified by suspect name.

Olivia:

This is a sample of text typed using the typewriter found in Olivia's house.

Christopher:

This is a sample of text typed using the typewriter found in Christopher's house.

Savannah:

This is a sample of text typed using the typewriter found in Savannah's house.

Ashley:

This is a sample of text typed using the typewriter found in Ashley's house.

Steven:

This is a sample of text typed using the typewriter found in Steven's house.

Karen:

This is a sample of text typed using the typewriter found in Karen's house.

Diana:

This is a sample of text typed using the typewriter found in Diana's house.

Glenn:

This is a sample of text typed using the typewriter found in Glenn's house.

Gerry:

This is a sample of text typed using the typewriter found in Gerry's house.

Think Ink: Ink Chromatography Lab
Teacher Instructions

Objective:

The student will learn that the inks in different pens have distinctive bands of color and that ink chromatography can be used to determine which pen was used to write a note.

Background Research:

Ink analysis may be used in a variety of situations. Investigators may analyze the ink used to write ransom notes, checks, wills, and other legal documents to determine if the documents have been altered or to determine the type of pen used in writing the document.

Different types of pens will write in different shades of ink depending on the manufacturer of the ink. Think about writing with a blue pen. Some blue pens write in a dark blue color, while others are light blue in color. Blue pens from different manufacturers will use different shades of blue ink. The same is true for black ink. Black pens will write in different shades of black depending on the manufacture of the ink used in the pen. Colored markers will have color variations in the same way that colored ink pens do.

Most inks are made up of a mixture of several organic dyes. It is the composition of this mixture that accounts for the different shades of ink color. Even though the inks may look similar, it is possible to tell the difference between the types of ink by using a process called ink chromatography. In this process, a sample spot of the ink is placed on a piece of absorbent or porous paper. The paper with the ink sample is put into a solvent such as water, acetone, or ethanol. As the solvent moves up the paper, it passes through the ink spot. Each component in the ink mixture travels up the paper and separates at different speeds. This leaves a band of colors on the paper that is different for each type of ink.

It is possible to determine which pen was used to write a note or other document by examining and comparing the bands of color between the known type of ink and the questioned ink.

Gathering Materials:

You will need four different pens or markers that write in black. One of the markers must be a Crayola washable marker. The thin-tipped markers work better. When dipped in acetone, the ink from the Crayola washable marker separates or runs into a variety of colors. It really doesn't matter what other pens you use. In addition to the Crayola marker, you could use a permanent marker, a transparency marker, and then a Bic or some other brand of ink pen. Test the pens you choose to see what kind of colors run before making your final selection.

You also will need thin strips of paper cut approximately 4 inches long and ¼ of an inch wide. (The strip needs to be long enough to be able to stick out of the test tube and skinny enough to fit inside the tube.) It is not necessary to use chromatography paper. Regular copy machine or printer paper works just as well.

You will need two glass test tubes and a test tube stand or something else that will hold the test tubes upright. Do not use plastic test tubes, as some chemicals will eat through or warp the plastic. Scotch tape, scissors, paper towels, and a prepared ransom note also are needed.

In this lab, the solvent used to process the ink is acetone. It can be purchased from a variety of companies (see Reference Materials on pp. 136–137).

Setting Up the Lab:

1. Choose four pens that write in black ink. One pen should be a Crayola washable marker. Test the other three pens to make sure they leave a unique mark when exposed to acetone.

2. Write in the name of the pens in the Pen Ownership Chart before making copies of the packet. It doesn't matter who owns which pen, however the owner of the Crayola marker will be the guilty party. For example, if one of the pens you are using is a Bic pen, write the word "Bic" in the box next to Danny's name.

3. Make copies of the Think Ink Student Lab on pages 88–91.

4. With the Crayola marker, write the following ransom note on a piece of white paper.

   We have your precious dog. If you ever wish to see your dog again, follow our directions exactly. Place $1,000 and three bags of M & Ms in a brown paper bag. Leave the bag under the slide at the playground at 8 p.m. tomorrow. Come alone.

5. If more than one class is participating in the lab, write one note for each class. Write the note in such a way that you can cut enough strips for all students to use a piece of the note. For example, if you will have 10 pairs of students completing the lab, make sure you can cut 10 horizontal strips from the note.

6. From the blank computer paper, cut strips of paper approximately 4 inches long and ¼ of an inch wide. The strip just needs to be long enough to be able to stick out of the test tube and skinny enough to fit inside the tube.

7. Pour a small amount of acetone into the glass test tube so that the height of the acetone in the test tube is approximately .5 cm. *Note:* Be sure to keep the amount of acetone under one centimeter as the students will be putting their ink spot at one centimeter on the paper. You do not want the ink spot to be sitting in the acetone. You want the acetone to crawl up the paper and through the ink. Place the filled test tubes in a test tube stand.

8. Place all materials at the chromatography station. Position the station in the room so that you can be near it to supervise the students.

Special Notes:

Although you could use five test tubes and get through the lab quicker, it is best to just use two at a time to allow the students to focus more attention on each individual pen test. It may be difficult for students to watch the ink running for five different pens at one time.

It is recommended that the teacher cut the paper strips from the ransom note. Students tend to cut big sections out of the note, thus not leaving enough of the sample for the rest of the class. Monitor the students closely and when they are in need of the sample from the note, cut a strip for them.

When doing the experiments in a station setting, remain near this lab and supervise it closely because students are working with chemicals. Although student contact with the acetone is very limited, accidents may occur. You may want to have students wear safety goggles while completing this lab.

Think Ink: Ink Chromatography Lab
Student Lab

Materials Needed:

Four black markers/pens, paper strips, two glass test tubes filled with acetone, scissors, paper towel, Scotch tape, ransom note

Essential Questions:

Do different pens have their own distinctive bands of color that make them unique? How can you determine which pen was used to write a note?

Background Research:

Ink analysis may be used in a variety of situations. Investigators may analyze the ink used to write ransom notes, checks, wills, and other legal documents to determine if the documents have been altered or to determine the type of pen used in writing the document.

Different types of pens will write in different shades of ink depending on the manufacturer of the ink. Think about writing with a blue pen. Some blue pens write in a dark blue color, while others are light blue in color. Blue pens from different manufacturers will use different shades of blue ink. The same is true for black ink. Black pens will write in different shades of black depending on the manufacture of the ink used in the pen. Colored markers will have color variations in the same way that colored ink pens do.

Most inks are made up of a mixture of several organic dyes. It is the composition of this mixture that accounts for the different shades of ink color. Even though the inks may look similar, it is possible to tell the difference between the types of ink by using a process called ink chromatography. In this process, a sample spot of the ink is placed on a piece of absorbent or porous paper. The paper with the ink sample is put into a solvent such as water, acetone, or ethanol. As the solvent moves up the paper, it passes through the ink spot. Each component in the ink mixture travels up the paper and separates at different speeds. This leaves a band of colors on the paper that is different for each type of ink.

It is possible to determine which pen was used to write a note or other document by examining and comparing the bands of color between the known type of ink and the questioned ink.

Crime Fighting Challenge

Matthew's prize show dog was "dognapped" on Tuesday. On Wednesday, Matthew found a handwritten note on his doorstep that said the following:

We have your precious dog. If you ever wish to see your dog again, follow our directions exactly. Place $1,000 and three bags of M & Ms in a brown paper bag. Leave the bag under the slide at the playground at 8 p.m. tomorrow. Come alone.

Matthew knows of four people who might have committed this dognapping. He suspects Danny, Jake, Eddie, or John. Police have questioned these four people and have taken a pen from each of the suspects. Follow the procedures below to determine which pen was used to write the note.

Experiment Procedures:

1. Select one of the four pens and write the name (or initial) of the pen at the top of a strip of paper. For example, if you use a Sharpie-brand marker, write an "S" or the word "Sharpie" at the end of one strip of paper. About 1 cm from the other end of the paper strip, place a small dot of the ink approximately 3 mm in diameter. Repeat this procedure for the other three pens.

2. Choose two of the marked strips of paper, and place them into separate test tubes containing acetone so that the ends with the ink dots go in first, but so that the ink dots do not touch the acetone. Take care not to let the paper strips touch the sides of the test tube or for the dot to go into the acetone. You want the acetone to "crawl" up the paper and through the ink dot. You do not want the ink dot to be soaking in the acetone.

3. Allow the acetone to move slowly up the papers. If you look closely, you will see the acetone creep up the paper. This may take a few minutes, so be patient. When the acetone hits and goes through the spot of ink, you will see the ink start to "bleed" and separate. After the acetone has gone 1 or 2 centimeters past the ink spot, remove the papers and place them on a paper towel to dry.

4. Repeat Steps 2 and 3 with the other two strips of papers.

5. Next, cut a thin strip of text from the ransom note or use the strip cut by your teacher. Put this strip into the acetone and follow the same procedures as above. The ink will react slightly different this time as the acetone has more "spots" of ink to go through as it passes through the different words on the note. When a color pattern is evident, remove the paper, place it on a paper towel and allow it to dry.

6. After all of the strips have dried, tape them in the designated box on the attached Chromatography Lab Results page.

7. Examine the different colors and tones in which the inks ran. Compare the results of the note test to the other pen tests. You should be able to determine the pen that wrote the ransom note by determining which two ink patterns match.

8. After you have identified which pen wrote the note, check the chart to see which suspect owned the pen.

CASE CLOSED

Based on your experiment results, which pen was used to write the ransom note? Who was responsible for dognapping Matthew's dog? Explain your answer.

_____

_____

_____

_____

_____

_____

_____

_____

_____

_____

_____

Chromatography Lab Results

Pen Ownership Chart	
Name of Suspect	**Type of Pen Owned**
Danny	
Jake	
Eddie	
John	

Tape your strips of paper here. On the line identify each sample (name of pen).

Strip 1 _____

Strip 2 _____

Strip 3 _____

Strip 4 _____

Strip 5 (Sample from ransom note)

If the Shoe Fits:
Shoe Print Impression Lab
Teacher Instructions

This lab is divided into two parts that are teacher directed. No student lab procedures sheet is needed. In Part I, students will make a plaster cast of their shoe impression. In Part II, students will match plaster casts to pictures of the shoes that made each impression.

Objective:

The student will make plaster casts of shoeprints and analyze the shoeprint casts in order to match them to the shoes that made the impressions.

Background Research:

There are two types of shoe prints. Some prints are left when a shoe leaves behind dusty, dirty, or oily residue on a surface. Other prints leave a depression as a result of stepping in soft ground or mud. Prints often are helpful in identifying a suspect. By examining the print, investigators often can determine the make, style, and size of the shoe. They also might be able to determine approximate weight, height, and gait of the owner of the shoe.

Shoe prints at a crime scene first are recorded by photograph. When photographing a shoe print, a ruler is included in the picture to help document the size of the shoe. Pictures are taken from several angles. Prints left in dusty or oily surfaces often can be lifted using the same procedures as lifting a fingerprint. In the case of a depression print, the depression is filled with plaster or dental stone. The cast is then removed and processed at the forensic lab.

Gathering Materials:

Part I. Students will be leaving a shoe impression in dirt. As a general guideline, you will need approximately 2 pounds of dirt per student, so a 40-pound bag of dirt would be enough for 20 students. Make sure you get dirt and not potting soil. Potting soil tends to have bits of mulch and other materials in it, which interfere with the quality of the print. You will need a small spade or gardening tool to use when putting dirt in the boxes.

You will need about one cup of powdered Plaster of Paris for each student. (It is a good idea to get a little extra for those students who might need a second batch.) Each student will need a quart-size resealable plastic bag, and a plastic cup that can hold about a cup of water. Students will be mixing the plaster and the water in the plastic bag, which makes for very easy clean up. You also will need a water source in your room or a pitcher of water (need about ⅔ of a cup of water for each student).

Popsicle sticks work great for smoothing out the plaster when it is poured into the shoe impression. They also come in handy when cleaning off the cast. Either supply the Popsicle sticks or ask students to bring one in. Toothbrushes and toothpicks also are helpful when cleaning the dirt off the solid cast. Ask each student to bring in an old toothbrush (never to be used again for teeth brushing!) and a few toothpicks. If you have funds available to purchase these items, go ahead and purchase enough for students to use.

If you have carpet in your classroom, you will need to cover it with a large tarp. It is much easier to clean off a tarp than carpet. If you have a tile floor, it may be easier to just sweep and wipe up the tile than to clean a tarp.

Ask each student to bring in a box that is large enough for his or her shoe to fit in. Shoeboxes work great as do shirt boxes. You also may want to collect the lids from boxes containing copy machine paper, as they are nice and sturdy. Collect these boxes prior to the day of the lab to ensure that students have a box when they need it. This also allows you to fill the boxes with dirt before the lab. Make sure the students write their name on the side of the box.

On the day of the lab, ask students to bring in or wear a shoe (from the right foot) with a unique sole that will leave distinct impressions. Tennis shoes work great if they are not so worn that you can't see unique patterns on the sole. Tell students they will be stepping in dirt so they don't want to bring in their best shoe. You may want to look at student shoes prior to the day of the lab and point out shoes that would leave good impressions.

You will need a digital camera to take pictures of the soles of the student shoes.

If students will be taking their casts home with them, it is a good idea to have old newspapers to wrap the cast in and a gallon-size plastic bag to put the cast in.

Part II. You will need to create a worksheet containing pictures of the soles of the shoes students wore when making their impressions. See Step 13 in Making the Casts and Step 1 in Cleaning, Comparing, and Identifying the Casts.

Setting Up the Lab:

Part I: Making the Casts

1. The day before the lab, fill the plastic bags with one cup of Plaster of Paris. You will need one bag for each student and a couple of extras for those students who may need a second one.

2. The day before or the morning of the lab, fill the plastic cups with approximately ⅔ of a cup of water—one for each student. Again, it is a good idea to have a few extra cups filled.

3. Before beginning the lab, prepare your classroom as necessary. This may mean placing a tarp over the carpet, and moving desks or tables to make room for students to work on the floor. This is something students can help you do before you begin the lab.

4. Put dirt in each student's box so that it is about 1 to 1½ inches thick. You need to have adequate dirt covering the bottom of the box so that when the student steps in the box to leave an impression there is still dirt under the shoe. You don't want the shoe print to be left on the bottom of the cardboard box as it won't allow unique marks to be left behind. A word about the dirt: The dirt needs to be slightly damp but not muddy. If you buy a bag of dirt and open it right before the lab, the dirt in the bag is usually slightly damp. If the dirt you are using is really dry, you may have to wet it slightly. Experiment with stepping in the dirt to see if it leaves an impression before making any adjustments to the moisture of the dirt. Do this prior to the lab.

5. When all boxes have been filled, ask the students to examine their dirt. They may need to break apart large clumps of dirt. They do not want to pack the soil down. It needs to be "loose" so that an impression can be made. Once the dirt has been prepared, ask the students to carefully step into their box with their right shoe. (You will want all right shoes for the purpose of comparing the casts later.) They will need to put their full weight on the shoe in the box to make sure a good impression is left. After they have made their impression, they should carefully remove their shoe from the box, and clean the dirt off of their shoe before going on to the next step.

6. Wait until all students have made their impression and then thoroughly explain the next few steps to the class before giving them the plaster materials. You may want to demonstrate the following procedures. Once students have their Plaster of Paris, they will need to act quickly so it does not harden too much.

7. Hand each student a bag filled with Plaster of Paris. Give them each a cup containing about ⅔ of a cup of water.

8. Have students pour the water into the bag of plaster and seal it tightly, leaving no air in the bag.

9. Students should begin kneading or squeezing the bag to thoroughly mix the plaster and the water. Here is the tricky part, so make sure students understand this. If they mix the plaster too long, it will harden and they won't be able to pour it out of their bag. If they don't mix it enough, it will be too runny. As a general rule, the Plaster of Paris should have the consistency of pancake batter. If a student's mixture is too runny, add a little more plaster. If it is too thick, try adding more water or just starting over with a new bag of plaster.

10. As soon as the mix is at an appropriate consistency, have the students open one corner of the bag and pour the mixture into their shoe impression. They should be close to the impression and fill the entire impression with the mix. They may use a Popsicle stick to help spread the mix around. They will not need to fill their entire box with the plaster. They should just fill the impression.

11. Once the impression is filled, have students throw away their plastic bag and cup.

12. The boxes containing the casts should be stored in a convenient location in your room. Give the casts several minutes to harden before moving the boxes. Students should take great care in moving their box as some of the casts tend to break. It is best if students can push or slide their box across the floor instead of picking it up. If they have to pick up the box they should support it carefully across the length of the box.

13. Before students leave, take a digital picture of the sole of the actual shoe they just made an impression of. Be sure to document the person who owns each shoe you photograph. These pictures will be used in the identification of the casts.

Part II: Cleaning, Comparing, and Identifying the Casts

1. Before beginning Part II of this lab, organize the pictures you took of the soles of the shoes (see Step 13) used for making an impression. One option that works well is to insert the pictures in a Word document. See sample worksheet on page 97. On the worksheet, do not identify who owns the shoe, simply number each picture. Below the picture leave a blank line where students can write the name of the person to whom the shoe belongs.

2. It is much easier to clean the dirt off the bottom of the cast if the dirt is dry. Therefore, allow several days for the dirt to dry before attempting to take the cast out of the box. Removing the casts the day after making them takes a lot more work to get the dirt off. You may wait as long as a week if you like.

3. When the casts have had adequate time to dry, students will remove the cast from the box of dirt. If you have carpeting in your room, be sure to place a

tarp on the carpeting. You may want to have students write their name on their cast before removing it. Students should start by digging in the dirt around the plaster cast, which will help loosen the cast. Students should continue to loosen the cast by using a Popsicle stick or their hands.

4. Once the cast has been removed from the dirt, the students will need to clean the dirt off of the cast. Popsicle sticks, toothpicks, and old toothbrushes work well for clearing the dirt away. Some students have even successfully run a small amount of water over the cast to take off any remaining dirt. The casts are easily broken so students should proceed carefully.

5. After cleaning the casts, have students place their cast, impression side up, in a designated area of the room. Each student should write his or her name next to his or her cast. *Note:* You may place several strips of bulletin board paper on the floor and have the students place their cast on this paper, writing their name next to the cast.

6. Distribute the worksheet containing the pictures of the actual soles of student shoes. Ask students to examine each picture and compare it to the casts in the room. Students should match the cast to the picture of the shoe that made the cast by looking for unique characteristics. When they have made a match, students should write the student name appearing next to the cast, on the line below the picture of the sole they believe made the cast.

7. Most students like to take their shoe casts home. Wrapping the cast in paper towels or newspapers and then placing it in a gallon size plastic bag is one safe way to get the cast home.

Special Notes:

Share the background research with students before beginning the lab.

This lab requires teacher instruction and isn't one that the students should do independently. You will need to be actively involved in all steps of the process. The lab is broken down into several small steps to keep the mess and chaos to a minimum. Having 40 pounds of dirt and 20 children in one room has the potential for being a disaster, but this is a favorite forensic lab and if organized correctly can result in a minimal amount of mess.

It is best to prepare as much of the lab as you can before students walk into the classroom, as it will make the lab run much more smoothly. It is just never a good idea to give a classroom full of students' boxes of dirt and expect them to wait patiently while the rest of the lab is being prepared.

Dental stone also may be used instead of Plaster of Paris. It is, however, more expensive to purchase.

Shoe Print Comparison
Sample Worksheet

Teachers, use this sample as a guide to making your own class shoe print worksheet.

Look at the plaster casts of the shoes placed in the room. Notice that each plaster cast is identified by the name of the person who owns the cast. Match the pictures on this page to the plaster cast of the shoe. Write the name of the person to whom the shoe belongs on the line provided.

Insert picture of student shoe here

Shoe #1 belongs to _____

Insert picture of student shoe here

Shoe #2 belongs to _____

Talking Bones: Forensic Anthropology Lab
Teacher Instructions

Objective:

The student will learn how to approximate a person's height based on the length of the person's tibia, fibula, or humerus bone.

Background Research:

Investigators are sometimes required to solve crimes involving human bones. Forensic anthropologists can study certain bones and determine approximate age, approximate height, gender, and race. This lab will explore using the length of bones to determine the approximate height of a victim. Three bones that scientists may use are the tibia, the fibula, and the humerus. The tibia is the inner, thicker leg bone located below the knee. The fibula is also located below the knee, but it is the long, thin, outer bone. The humerus is an arm bone located between the shoulder and elbow.

There is a correlation or relationship between the length of these bones and the height of a person. Scientists have developed tables to help them estimate the height of a person given the lengths of these bones (see Table 1). Different formulas have been developed for the different bones and for each gender (male or female). By using the formulas listed in the table, forensic anthropologists are able to approximate the height of a person generally within 4 centimeters. If race is known, scientists use a more specific chart for a particular race.

Table 1: Formulas to Figure Human Height by Bone Length

Bone	Male	Female
Fibula (lower leg)	(Fibula length × 2.44) + 78.36	(Fibula length × 2.71) + 65.26
Tibia (lower leg)	(Tibia length × 2.37) + 80.97	(Tibia length × 2.68) + 65.63
Humerus (upper arm)	(Humerus length × 2.99) + 72.42	(Humerus length × 3.22) + 61.32

For this purpose bones are measured in centimeters. Notice the table is organized by type of bone and by gender. A different formula is used for each.

After determining the length of a bone in centimeters, substitute that measurement for the bone length in the formula. Complete the formula calculations to determine the approximate height of the person in centimeters. Height is normally referred to in feet and inches, so after using the formula, convert your calculations from centimeters to feet and inches (1 inch = 2.54 cm). See examples in Figure 1.

Example 1: Calculating height in centimeters

A tibia measures 42 cm. Approximately how tall, in feet and inches, is the person to whom the tibia belongs?

Because we initially do not know if the bone belongs to a male or female we will need to complete the calculations for both genders. Choose the formulas for a tibia, substitute 42 for the tibia length, and complete the calculations.

Male	Female
(Tibia length $\times$ 2.37) + 80.97	(Tibia length $\times$ 2.68) + 65.63
(42 x 2.37) + 80.97=	(42 x 2.68) + 65.63 =
99.54 + 80.97 =	112.56 + 65.63 =
180.51 cm	178.19 cm

Based on the calculations, a tibia measuring 42 cm long would belong to a male approximately 181 cm tall or a female 178 cm tall. Convert these answers to feet and inches by following these steps: Divide your centimeter answer by 2.54 and then round to the nearest whole number (to simplify matters). This gives you the approximate height in inches. Then divide by 12 (inches) to change your answer to feet and inches. See Example 2.

Example 2: Converting centimeters to feet and inches

Male	Female
180.51 ÷ 2.54 cm = 71 inches (rounded)	178.19 ÷ 2.54 cm = 70 inches (rounded)
71 ÷ 12 inches = 5 with a remainder of 11	70 ÷ 12 inches = 5 with a remainder of 10
5 feet 11 inches	5 feet 10 inches

The bone could belong to a male approximately 5 feet 11 inches or a female 5 feet 10 inches tall.

Figure 1. Examples of using the bone length to height formula.

Gathering Materials:

In Experiment 1, the students will need a copy of the student lab (pp. 104–107) and a calculator. For Experiment 2, students will need a copy of the student lab (pp. 108–109), a metric ruler or meter stick, a calculator, and the drawings of the simulated bones (pp. 110–111). Instead of using the drawings of the bones, you may also choose to purchase and use simulated bones. (See Reference Materials on pp. 136–137.)

Optional Quiz:

Before beginning the lab, tell students it is important for a forensic scientist to be able to identify an isolated bone by name. Give them a note sheet containing a diagram of a human skeleton on which the various bones are labeled by name (see p. 102). Students are to memorize the bones and identify them on a quiz (see p. 103).

Setting Up the Lab:

1. Make copies of the two student labs (pp. 104–109), one for each student or one per group of students. It seems to be less confusing for the kids if the worksheets for Experiments 1 and 2, along with the introductory page, are copied together as one packet.

2. Read through "Background Research" and discuss the formula for figuring height and weight with the students and then work through several examples of calculating approximate heights with the class prior to allowing the students to work through the lab independently. Some may struggle with the mathematical concepts. Giving them guided practice before the lab makes it easier to complete the lab independently.

3. Make copies of the bones on pages 110–111. You will not necessarily need a copy for every student. You may make a set for each station you have set up.

4. If you will be using simulated bones instead of the drawings, place those bones at the experiment station.

5. Be sure to have a metric ruler or meter stick and calculators available for student use.

6. Place all materials at the anthropology station.

Special Notes:

Although scientists are exact in their measurements, it may be easier for the students to round their calculations. Calculations are rounded when converting from centimeters to inches in the example provided on the student worksheet. Students usually have no difficulty in using the formulas but many do struggle with converting their answers from centimeters to feet and inches. Requiring students to show each step helps them better understand the mathematical process. When dividing inches by feet it is easiest to have students do the work on paper and not use a calculator. Using a calculator gives a decimal answer, which makes it harder to convert.

Dividing the "long" way shows students that any remainder left represents inches. Take, for example, the problem 63 ÷ 12: 12 divides into 63 five times with 3 leftover. The 5 represents the number of feet while the 3 leftover represents the number of inches. So, 63 ÷ 12 = 5 feet 3 inches. Demonstrate several examples to the class before having them complete the lab independently.

Scientists may use a variety of bones (femur, tibia, humerus, radius, fibula) to determine the approximate height of a person. On the student worksheet, I chose to use the humerus, fibula, and tibia because I had purchased those simulated bones from the Carolina Biological Supply Company. If you have access to simulated bones, you may have the students measure those for the second experiment instead of using the drawings in the book. Another idea would be to use actual x-rays of the particular bones for student measurements. I also have discovered in my research that the formulas for approximating height vary slightly from source to source. For this particular lab, I used the formulas that were included in the information that came with the simulated bones.

Diagram of a Human Skeleton

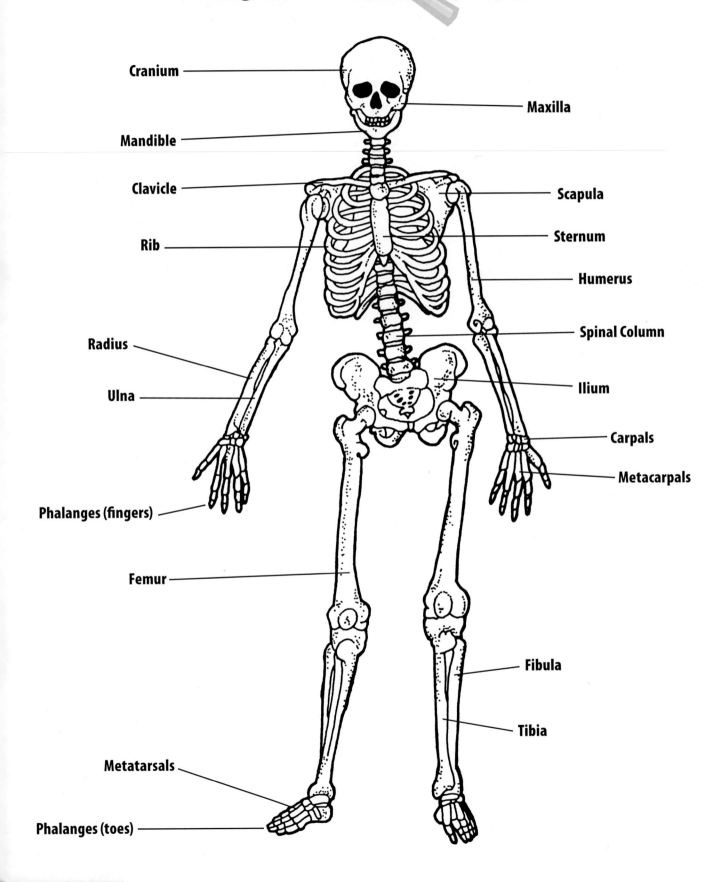

Cranium

Maxilla

Mandible

Clavicle

Scapula

Rib

Sternum

Humerus

Radius

Spinal Column

Ulna

Ilium

Carpals

Metacarpals

Phalanges (fingers)

Femur

Fibula

Tibia

Metatarsals

Phalanges (toes)

Name:_____ Date:_____

Skeleton Quiz

Use the skeleton diagram that is provided. Match the corresponding number on the skeleton diagram to the name of the bone from the list below. (You will use the term phalanges twice.)

_____ 1.   A. Carpals

_____ 2.   B. Clavicle

_____ 3.   C. Cranium

_____ 4.   D. Femur

_____ 5.   E. Fibula

_____ 6.   F. Humerus

_____ 7.   G. Ilium

_____ 8.   H. Mandible

_____ 9.   I. Maxilla

_____ 10.   J. Metacarpals

_____ 11.   K. Metatarsals

_____ 12.   L. Phalanges (use this word twice)

_____ 13.   M. Radius

_____ 14.   N. Rib

_____ 15.   O. Scapula

_____ 16.   P. Spinal Column

_____ 17.   Q. Sternum

_____ 18.   R. Tibia

_____ 19.   S. Ulna

_____ 20.

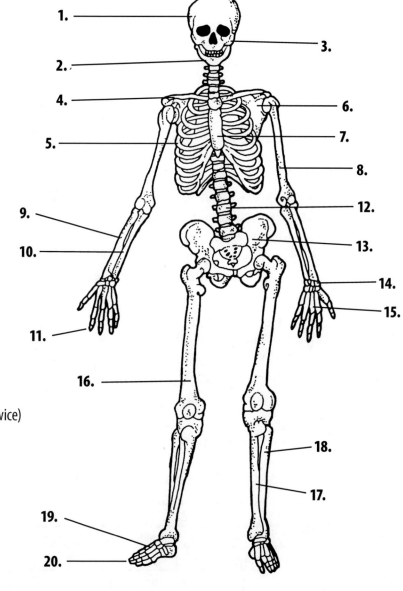

Name:_____ **Date:**_____

Talking Bones: Forensic Anthropology
Student Lab

Materials Needed:

Experiment 1: calculator; Experiment 2: printed handouts containing drawings of humerus and fibula bones or simulated bones, metric ruler, calculator

Essential Question:

How can you determine the height of a person given a tibia, fibula, or humerus bone?

Background Research:

Investigators are sometimes required to solve crimes involving human bones. Forensic anthropologists can study certain bones and determine approximate age, approximate height, gender, and race. This lab will explore using the length of bones to determine the approximate height of a victim. Three bones that scientists may use are the tibia, the fibula, and the humerus. The tibia is the inner, thicker leg bone located below the knee. The fibula is also located below the knee, but it is the long, thin, outer bone. The humerus is an arm bone located between the shoulder and elbow.

There is a correlation or relationship between the length of these bones and the height of a person. Scientists have developed tables to help them estimate the height of a person given the lengths of these bones (see Table 1). Different formulas have been developed for the different bones and for each gender (male or female). By using the formulas listed in the table, forensic anthropologists are able to approximate the height of a person generally within 4 centimeters. If race is known, scientists use a more specific chart for a particular race.

Table 1: Formulas to Figure Human Height by Bone Length

Bone	Male	Female
Fibula (lower leg)	(Fibula length × 2.44) + 78.36	(Fibula length × 2.71) + 65.26
Tibia (lower leg)	(Tibia length × 2.37) + 80.97	(Tibia length × 2.68) + 65.63
Humerus (upper arm)	(Humerus length × 2.99) + 72.42	(Humerus length × 3.22) + 61.32

For this purpose bones are measured in centimeters. Notice the table is organized by type of bone and by gender. A different formula is used for each.

After determining the length of a bone in centimeters, substitute that measurement for the bone length in the formula. Complete the formula calculations to determine the approximate height of the person in centimeters.

Height is normally referred to in feet and inches, so after using the formula, convert your calculations from centimeters to feet and inches (1 inch = 2.54 cm). See examples in Figure 5. Refer back to these steps as necessary to complete Experiments 1 and 2.

Example 1: Calculating height in centimeters

A tibia measures 42 cm. Approximately how tall, in feet and inches, is the person to whom the tibia belongs?

Because we initially do not know if the bone belongs to a male or female, we will need to complete the calculations for both genders. Choose the formulas for a tibia, substitute 42 for the tibia length, and complete the calculations.

Male	Female
(Tibia length $\times$ 2.37) + 80.97	(Tibia length $\times$ 2.68) + 65.63
(42 x 2.37) + 80.97=	(42 x 2.68) + 65.63 =
99.54 + 80.97 =	112.56 + 65.63 =
180.51 cm	178.19 cm

Based on the calculations, a tibia measuring 42 cm long would belong to a male approximately 181 cm tall or a female 178 cm tall. Convert these answers to feet and inches by following these steps: Divide your centimeter answer by 2.54 and then round to the nearest whole number (to simplify matters). This gives you the approximate height in inches. Then divide by 12 (inches) to change your answer to feet and inches. See Example 2.

Example 2: Converting centimeters to feet and inches

Male	Female
180.51 ÷ 2.54 cm = 71 inches (rounded)	178.19 ÷ 2.54 cm = 70 inches (rounded)
71 ÷ 12 inches = 5 with a remainder of 11	70 ÷ 12 inches = 5 with a remainder of 10
5 feet 11 inches	5 feet 10 inches

The bone could belong to a male approximately 5 feet 11 inches or a female 5 feet 10 inches tall.

Figure 1. Examples of using the bone length to height formula.

Talking Bones: Forensic Anthropology
Student Lab: Experiment 1

The Missouri Homebuilders Company was beginning construction of a new subdivision in the outskirts of the city of Ballwin. As workers were digging the basement of a home, they discovered two bones that appeared to be human. Police investigators arrived and processed the scene. The bones were recovered and analyzed in a local forensic lab. Forensic anthropologists examined the two bones and determined one was a humerus measuring 40 centimeters long and the other was a fibula measuring 35 centimeters long. Four people in the area had been reported missing in the past year. The missing persons are:

Reported Missing	Height (ft. and in.)
Ryan Wegener	6' 3"
Cheryl Hartmann	5' 3"
Chelsea Moll	5' 10"
Robbie Graber	5' 11"

Follow the experiment procedures to determine, based on the length of the recovered bones, to whom the bones might belong.

Experiment Procedures:

1. Record your work in the boxes provided.

2. Refer back to the Background Research section as necessary for formulas and examples.

3. Choose the correct formula for determining height based on the type of bone and gender.

4. Substitute in the measurements in centimeters of the humerus and the fibula.

5. Calculate the equations to determine the approximate height for a male and female. Be sure to convert your centimeter answer to feet and inches.

6. Compare your findings to the heights of the missing persons identified in the table above to determine to whom the bones might belong.

Humerus	
Male	**Female**

Fibula	
Male	**Female**

CASE CLOSED

Based on your experiment results, to whom might the humerus belong? To whom might the fibula belong? Explain how you arrived at your answers.

_____

_____

_____

_____

Talking Bones: Forensic Anthropology
Student Lab: Experiment 2

Crime Fighting Challenge

Two bones were recovered from a shallow grave near the site of an archaeological dig. One bone is a humerus and the other bone is a tibia. Police are trying to determine the identity of the person(s) to whom the bones belong. They need to determine if the bones belong to the same person or if they come from two different people.

By using the formulas for approximating height, you can help the police solve this case. Follow the experiment procedures to determine if the bones could belong to the same person or two different people.

Experiment Procedures:

1. Use a metric ruler or meter stick to measure the bones to the nearest centimeter. Record your answers in the box below.

A. The humerus bone measures (to the nearest centimeter):

B. The tibia bone measures (to the nearest centimeter):

2. Choose the correct formulas for the humerus, and complete the calculations to determine the approximate height for a male and female. Be sure to write your final answer in terms of feet and inches. Show your work in the box below.

Humerus	
Male	**Female**

3. Choose the correct formulas for the tibia, and complete the calculations to determine the approximate height for a male and female. Be sure to write your final answer in terms of feet and inches. Show your work in the box below.

Tibia	
Male	**Female**

CASE CLOSED

Given the approximate height of the male and female, who could own these bones? Based on your experiment results, could the bones belong to the same person or did they come from two different people? Explain how you arrived at your answer.

_____

_____

_____

_____

_____

_____

_____

_____

_____

_____

Humerus

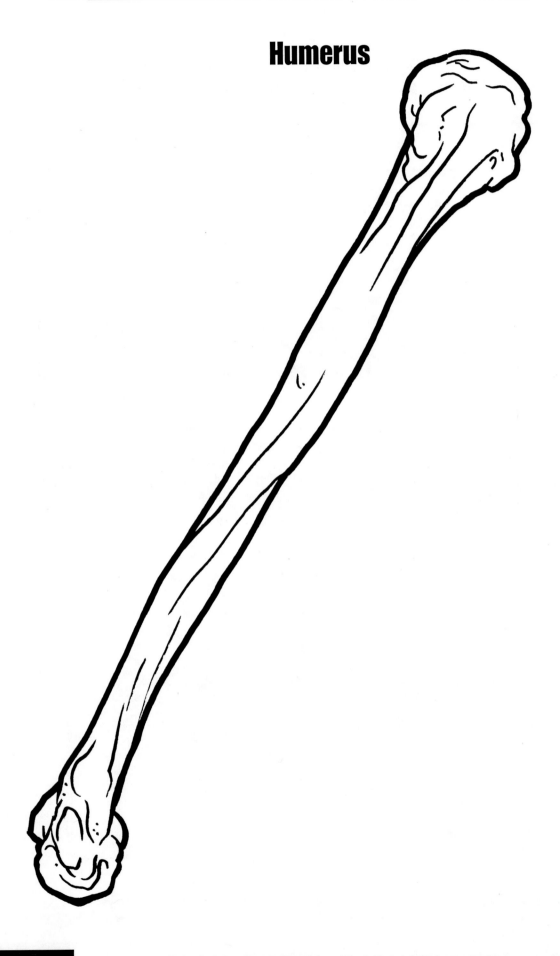

Tibia

Seeing Red: Blood Spatter Labs
Teacher Instructions

Objective:

The student will learn how blood spatter patterns are affected by drop height and the surface on which they land, and how they may be used in criminal investigations to determine angle of impact.

Background Research:

Forensic scientists examine bloodstain patterns to help determine the events surrounding a crime scene involving blood spatter. The unique arrangement of the blood spatter can tell a story. In simplest terms, blood spatter is just a collection of blood spots that may be different sizes and shapes that are formed by a variety of methods.

Blood will spatter when an outside force breaks the surface tension of a blood drop. In other words, blood will not spatter until it hits a surface. Blood spatter is typically in the shape of an ellipse (a closed plane curve like an oval or circle). The type of surface the blood hits will influence the shape of the blood drops. In general, when blood hits a hard, smooth, nonporous surface, it will create very little spatter so the edges of the blood spatter will be round and smooth. When blood hits a porous, rough surface, it tends to spatter more so the drops of blood will be jagged or have spikes around the edges. See examples below:

Nonporous, smooth surface   **Porous, rough surface**

In addition to the surface influencing the shape of the spatter, the angle at which blood hits a surface also will determine the shape. For example, blood that hits a wall at a 90° angle will be circular in shape. Blood that hits a wall at a 20° angle will be long and thin. The closer you get to 90° angle of impact, the more circular the spatter will be. See examples below:

Blood spatter with a 90° angle of impact   **Blood spatter with a 20° angle of impact**

The size of the blood spatter will change as the distance from which the blood hits a surface changes. The further away the blood is before it hits a surface, the larger the individual drops of blood spatter will be.

It is possible to determine the angle at which a blood shedding event, such as a gunshot wound, occurred. Mathematically speaking, the width and length of an ellipse have a unique relationship. By figuring out the ratio of the two and using the trigonometric function sine, scientists are able to determine the angle of impact at which the blood spatter occurred. This information can help investigators recreate a crime scene or confirm a suspect or victim's story. Look at the following example:

The width of the blood spatter above is 16 mm and the length is 24 mm. To determine the ratio between the two, divide the width by the length. Convert the ratio to an angle measure using a table of trigonometric ratios (see Table 1 on p. 125) or by using the sine function on a scientific calculator.

Steps to follow when using a trigonometric table:

1. Divide 16 by 24 (.6667).

2. Look at the table and find the number .6667 under the Sine column.

3. The number falls between .6561 and .6691 on the table. It is closer to .6691.

4. .6691 corresponds to the angle measure 42.

If you are going to calculate the angle using a calculator, follow the directions in your calculator manual for the sine function.

In conclusion, blood spatter that is 16 mm wide and 24 mm long hits the surface at approximately a 42° angle.

The study of blood spatter patterns can be a valuable tool for helping investigators recreate a crime scene involving a blood shedding event.

Please note that in the labs that follow, your students will be measuring a variety of blood spatter samples. Because it is difficult to measure a photocopied image precisely, your students' answers may differ slightly from the answer key. You may want to show students how to draw straight lines at the furthest points of the spatters' lengths and widths to aid in measurement. You also will want to make sure the photocopy machine you use does not scale down the page images, or adjust the answer key to fit your copy's scaling.

Seeing Red: Blood Spatter Lab 1: Surface-Shape Relationship
Teacher Instructions

Gathering Materials:

Simulated blood, eyedroppers, and newspapers are needed. Although recipes exist for making your own simulated blood, the experiments work best by using commercially prepared simulated blood. This blood is relatively inexpensive and can be purchased at several science supply companies. See Reference Materials on pages 136–137.

The surfaces chosen for this lab are a carpet square, glass (a picture frame or free standing window), a ceramic tile (smooth, nonporous), corrugated cardboard, a fabric swatch, and a sponge. You may substitute other surfaces as you wish. Your items should be large enough so that a student can hit them with a drop of blood from 12 inches away. You also will need student copies of the Blood Spatter Lab 1 on pages 115–117.

Setting Up the Lab:

1. Make copies of the student lab on pages 115–117.

2. Prepare the work area by covering it with newspaper.

3. Place the surface materials at the station.

4. Along with an eyedropper, place a small amount of simulated blood in a small plastic cup at each station.

Special Notes:

Demonstrate the correct way to drop a sample of blood. Holding the eyedropper 12 inches above the surface is high enough to do the trick. Advise students that the simulated blood may stain fabrics and that they should take great care in working with this liquid. You may want to provide plastic aprons or smocks to help protect student clothing.

You will need at most 12 drops of blood per group for this lab, which will allow students to try dropping the blood twice to each surface if they choose to do so. Limit the amount of blood you place at the station to minimize the chance of spills. You can always refill the cup as necessary.

Monitor students during the lab to make sure they are using the materials appropriately and that they are completing the required chart correctly.

Seeing Red: Blood Spatter Lab 1: Surface-Shape Relationship
Student Lab 1

Materials Needed:

Simulated blood, eyedropper, newspaper, carpet square, glass, ceramic tile, cardboard, fabric, sponge

Essential Question:

How does the texture of a surface, both porous and nonporous, affect the shape of blood spatter?

Background Research:

Forensic scientists examine bloodstain patterns to help determine the events surrounding a crime scene involving blood spatter. The unique arrangement of the blood spatter can tell a story. In simplest terms, blood spatter is just a collection of blood spots that may be different sizes and shapes that are formed by a variety of methods.

Blood will spatter when an outside force breaks the surface tension of a blood drop. Blood will not spatter until it hits a surface. Blood spatter is typically in the shape of an ellipse (an oval or circle). The type of surface the blood hits will influence the shape of blood drops. When blood hits a hard, smooth, nonporous surface, it will create very little spatter so the edges of the drops will be round and smooth. When blood hits a porous, rough surface, it tends to spatter more so the drops will be jagged or have spikes around the edges. See examples below:

Nonporous, smooth surface   **Porous, rough surface**

Every crime scene brings new challenges to investigators, who must rely on their previous experiences and knowledge to help them work and solve a case. After completing the experiment procedures below, use your gained knowledge to make predictions about blood spatter shape on a new list of surfaces. Be prepared to justify your predictions.

Crime Fighting Challenge

Experiment Procedures:

Caution: Simulated blood may stain fabrics and other materials. Take great care not to get any of the liquid on your clothing. Make sure your work area is covered with newspaper before beginning the lab.

1. Place the various surfaces on the newspaper. If you do not have room for all of the materials, then you will need to complete the experiment by placing one surface type on the newspaper at a time.

2. Fill the eyedropper with simulated blood. Make sure to clear the dropper of any air bubbles.

3. Hold the eyedropper approximately one foot above the surface and then squeeze a drop of blood onto the surface. Sketch the shape of the resulting spatter in the chart provided. You may repeat the test for this surface by dropping another drop of blood. Do this carefully to avoid dropping the blood in the same spot as the first drop.

4. Repeat steps 2 and 3 using the other surfaces.

5. Complete the Blood Spatter Surface-Shape Chart on the next page as you conduct the experiment. Identify each type of surface as porous or nonporous and then sketch the spatter as it appears on each specific surface.

CASE CLOSED

Based on your observations, predict what the shape of the blood spatter will be (smooth or jagged edges) if blood is dropped on the following surfaces: a plastic CD case, a sidewalk, a newspaper, the hood of a car, and a paper towel. Justify your predictions using specific information from the lab.

_____

_____

_____

_____

_____

_____

_____

_____

_____

_____

Name:_____ Date:_____

Blood Spatter Surface-Shape Chart

Type of Surface	Porous or Nonporous	Sketch of Blood Spatter
Carpet Square		
Glass		
Ceramic Tile		
Cardboard		
Fabric		
Sponge		

Seeing Red: Blood Spatter Lab 2: Distance-Shape Relationship
Teacher Instructions

Gathering Materials:

Simulated blood, eyedroppers, and newspapers are needed. In addition, each station or group of students will need a clipboard, computer paper, a yardstick, and a metric ruler. You also will need student copies of the Blood Spatter Lab 2 on pages 119–121.

Setting Up the Lab:

1. Make copies of the student lab on pages 119–121.

2. Prepare the work area by covering it with newspaper.

3. Place a clipboard, yardstick, and metric ruler at each station.

4. Each group will need a sheet of paper. If students will be rotating through a station, leave enough paper at the station to accommodate all groups.

5. Along with an eyedropper, place a small amount of simulated blood in a small plastic cup at each station.

6. Students will need to angle the clipboard. You may choose to place a pile of books or other materials at the station so that students can lean the clipboard against the books to create an angle or incline. Be sure to cover the books with newspaper.

Special Notes:

Advise students that the simulated blood may stain fabrics and that they should take great care in working with this liquid.

You will need at most eight drops of blood per group for this lab, which will allow students to try dropping the blood twice from each distance. Limit the amount of blood you place at the station to minimize the chance of spills. You can always refill the cup as necessary.

No matter how far away from the surface the blood is dropped, the overall shape of the blood spatter will remain the same. Although the size of the spatter will increase the further away the blood is dropped, the shapes will remain similar.

Seeing Red: Blood Spatter Lab 2: Distance-Shape Relationship
Student Lab 2

Materials Needed:

Simulated blood, eyedropper, newspaper, clipboard, paper, yardstick, metric ruler

Essential Question:

How does the distance associated with the impact of blood to a surface affect the size of the blood spatter?

Background Research:

Forensic scientists examine bloodstain patterns to help determine the events surrounding a crime scene involving blood spatter. The unique arrangement of the blood spatter can tell a story. In simplest terms, blood spatter is just a collection of blood spots that may be different sizes and shapes that are formed by a variety of methods.

Blood will spatter when an outside force breaks the surface tension of a blood drop. In other words, blood will not spatter until it hits a surface. Blood spatter is typically in the shape of an ellipse (a closed plane curve like an oval or circle). The distance from which blood hits a surface will determine the size of the blood spatter.

Crime Fighting Challenge

As a bloodstain expert, you have been called by the prosecuting attorney to testify in court in the case of the State vs. Christopher Stryker. Here are the specifics about the case. Sam Smith was shot in the shoulder, resulting in large blood spatter patterns being visible against a wall. Christopher Stryker, the man who was charged with shooting Sam, claims that the two of them struggled and were up against the wall when the gun accidentally fired. Sam claims Chris shot him while he, Sam, was standing about 4 feet away from the wall and that no struggle took place. You have examined the bloodstain patterns and have determined that they are quite large in nature. Follow the experiment procedures below to determine if large spatter patterns indicate close or distant range.

Experiment Procedures:

Caution: Simulated blood may stain fabrics and other materials. Take great care not to get any of the liquid on your clothing.

1. Make sure your work area is covered with newspaper before beginning the lab.

2. Place a piece of paper on the clipboard. Place the clipboard at an angle (approximately 45°) by leaning it against a stack of books or other materials provided by your teacher. (*Note*: No matter what you use to angle the clipboard make sure you cover the materials with newspaper.)

3. Fill the eyedropper with simulated blood. Make sure to clear the dropper of any air bubbles.

4. Hold a yardstick so it is standing on its end on the table next to the clipboard. Using the yardstick as a guide, drop one drop of the simulated blood from the 6-inch mark on the yardstick. Note the size and shape of the spatter. Label this drop 6 on the paper.

5. Repeat this procedure dropping one drop of simulated blood from the 16-inch mark, the 26-inch mark, and the 36-inch mark, taking care not to drop blood on an existing drop. Label each drop 16, 26, and 36 respectively.

6. Remove the paper from the clipboard. Observe the blood spatter marks made on the paper. Using a metric ruler, take measurements of the length and width of each drop. Because the spatter may still be wet, you may just hold the ruler over the drops to estimate the required measurements. Write the length and width of the four drops here, categorizing the measurements by the height of the drop.

Distance Blood Was Dropped	Length of Spatter in mm	Width of Spatter in mm
6 inches		
16 inches		
26 inches		
36 inches		

7. What is the relationship between the size of the blood spatter and the distance from which it is dropped? (In other words, how did the size of the blood spatter change as the distance from which the blood was dropped increased?) Record your conclusions here.

_____

_____

_____

8. Examine the shapes of each blood drop. Did the height from which you dropped the blood change the shape (not size) of the spatter? Explain by describing the shapes of each blood spatter.

_____

_____

_____

CASE CLOSED

The initial investigation revealed blood spatters that were large in size. Based on the conclusions you drew from completing the experiment, what will be your testimony in court? Was the shot fired at close or distant range? Will you support Chris' story or Sam's story? Be sure to answer all questions justifying your answer with facts from your research.

_____

_____

_____

_____

_____

_____

_____

_____

Seeing Red: Blood Spatter Lab 3: Angle of Impact

Teacher Instructions

Gathering Materials:

To complete this lab, students will need calculators, metric rulers, and a table of trigonometric ratios. They also will need student copies of the Blood Spatter Lab 3 on pages 124–127 and the blood drop samples on page 128.

Setting Up the Lab:

1. Make copies of the student lab on pages 124–127 and the blood drop samples on page 128.

2. Discuss the mathematics involved in the lab before having the students work the problems on their own. Explain the relationship between the width and the length of an ellipse. You can hand out the student lab sheet and read through the problems with the students or just model examples you have created.

3. Demonstrate how to measure the length and width of a drop of blood spatter. Measuring in millimeters is the most accurate and easiest unit to use.

4. Demonstrate how to use the trigonometric table or how to use a calculator to determine a sine function.

5. Show students how this information may help investigators in a crime scene. Draw three blood spatter patterns on the chalkboard. Calculate the angle of impact for each one. Attach a separate piece of string to the middle of each spatter. Using a protractor with the flat edge placed perpendicular against the board, hold the string out and away from the board at the angle of calculated impact. Do this for each spatter. Holding all three strings out at the same time, determine where the strings meet. This is where the impact occurred to create the spatter on the board. This can help investigators recreate a crime scene. For example, they may be able to determine where a victim was standing when he was shot. See Figure 1.

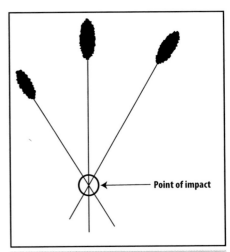

Figure 1. Point of impact of blood spatters.

6. If students are rotating through stations, you may just place the blood spatter sample pages at the station or you may choose to run a copy of the samples for each student and distribute them to everyone in the class at the same time.

Special Notes:

When students have finished the lab, you may want to cut the samples apart and put them in ascending order by angle of impact so students can see the spatter progress from a long, skinny oval to an almost perfect circle.

You may want to make your own blood spatter patterns with the simulated blood used in the first two labs. Take a large unlined note card or a sheet of stock paper and place it on a clipboard. Angle the clipboard and squeeze a drop of blood on the card. Remove the card to dry. Repeat this procedure with a new note card, angling the clipboard at a different angle each time. Vary the angles so that you have spatter ranging from 10° to 90° producing spatter appearing long and thin in shape to circular in shape.

Remember the closer to 90° the clipboard is (meaning the clipboard is lying flat on the table), the more circular the shape. The closer to 10° the clipboard is (meaning the clipboard is angled almost vertical to the table), the more elongated the shape.

Seeing Red: Blood Spatter Lab 3: Angle of Impact
Student Lab 3

Materials Needed:

Metric ruler, calculator, trigonometric table, blood spatter samples

Essential Question:

How does the shape of blood spatter determine the angle of impact?

Background Research:

Forensic scientists examine bloodstain patterns to help determine the events surrounding a crime scene involving blood spatter. The unique arrangement of the blood spatter can tell a story. Blood spatter is just a collection of blood spots that may be different sizes and shapes formed by a variety of methods.

Blood will spatter when an outside force breaks the surface tension of a blood drop. In other words, blood will not spatter until it hits a surface. Blood spatter is typically in the shape of an ellipse (a closed plane curve like an oval or circle). Mathematically speaking, the width and length of an ellipse have a unique relationship. By figuring out the ratio of the two and using a trigonometric function, scientists can determine the angle of impact at which the blood spatter occurred. This can help investigators recreate a crime scene or confirm a suspect or victim's story. Look at the following example:

The width of the blood spatter above is 16 mm and the length is 24 mm. To determine the ratio between the two, divide the width by the length. Convert the ratio to an angle measure using a table of trigonometric ratios (see Table 1) or by using the sine function on a scientific calculator.

Steps to follow when using a trigonometric table:

1. Divide 16 by 24 (.6667).

2. Look at the chart and find the number .6667 under the Sine column.

3. The number falls between .6561 and .6691 on the table. It is closer to .6691.

4. .6691 corresponds to the angle measure 42.

If you are going to calculate the angle using a calculator, follow the directions in your calculator manual for the sine function.

In conclusion, blood spatter that is 16 mm wide and 24 mm long hit the surface at approximately a 42° angle.

Table 1. Table of Trigonometric Ratios

Angle	Sine	Angle	Sine	Angle	Sine	Angle	Sine	Angle	Sine	Angle	Sine
1	0.0175	16	0.2756	31	0.5150	46	0.7193	61	0.8746	76	0.9703
2	0.0349	17	0.2924	32	0.5299	47	0.7314	62	0.8829	77	0.9744
3	0.0523	18	0.3090	33	0.5446	48	0.7431	63	0.8910	78	0.9781
4	0.0698	19	0.3256	34	0.5592	49	0.7547	64	0.8988	79	0.9816
5	0.0872	20	0.3420	35	0.5736	50	0.7660	65	0.9063	80	0.9848
6	0.1045	21	0.3584	36	0.5878	51	0.7771	66	0.9135	81	0.9877
7	0.1219	22	0.3746	37	0.6018	52	0.7880	67	0.9205	82	0.9903
8	0.1392	23	0.3907	38	0.6157	53	0.7986	68	0.9272	83	0.9925
9	0.1564	24	0.4067	39	0.6293	54	0.8090	69	0.9336	84	0.9945
10	0.1736	25	0.4226	40	0.6428	55	0.8192	70	0.9397	85	0.9962
11	0.1908	26	0.4384	41	0.6561	56	0.8290	71	0.9455	86	0.9976
12	0.2079	27	0.4540	42	0.6691	57	0.8387	72	0.9511	87	0.9986
13	0.2250	28	0.4695	43	0.6820	58	0.8480	73	0.9563	88	0.9994
14	0.2419	29	0.4848	44	0.6947	59	0.8572	74	0.9613	89	0.9998
15	0.2588	30	0.5000	45	0.7071	60	0.8660	75	0.9659	90	1.0000

Crime Fighting Challenge

As a blood spatter expert you have been called upon to examine pictures of a crime scene in which a person was shot. In the pictures the blood spatter is in the shape of almost perfect circles. Here are a few facts from the accompanying police report. Bob was shot by Rob. Bob and Rob are the same height. Rob's testimony claims Bob attacked him. Rob fell to the floor during the struggle. As Bob walked toward him, Rob fired the gun in self-defense while he was still lying on the ground. Bob, having survived the shot, claims the two men were standing face to face when Rob fired the gun. Based on the shape of the blood spatter, who is telling the truth? Justify your answer. Follow the experiment procedures to help you determine who is telling the truth.

Experiment Procedures:

1. Using a metric ruler, measure the length and width of a blood drop spatter appearing on the Simulated Blood Drop Samples handout. Record the measurements in the appropriate row on the Determining the Angle of Impact chart provided.

2. Divide the width by the length to get a decimal answer (round to the nearest ten-thousandths) and record this in the appropriate ratio column.

3. Change this ratio into the corresponding angle measure by using the SINE function on a scientific calculator or by locating the ratio on a trigonometric table on page 125 or one provided by your teacher. Record this number in the appropriate column.

4. Repeat this procedure for the remaining blood spatter samples.

5. Look at the samples. Note the shapes of the blood spatter. The more circular the blood drop, the closer the angle of impact is to 90°. The longer and skinnier the blood drop, the closer to 10° it is.

Determining the Angle of Impact

Sample Number	Width (in mm)	Length (in mm)	Ratio (as a Decimal)	Angle of Impact in Degrees
1.				
2.				
3.				
4.				
5.				
6.				
7.				
8.				

CASE CLOSED

Who is telling the truth, Bob or Rob? Did Rob fire the gun from a standing position or from lying on the floor? Be sure to explain how you determined the angle at which the gun was fired when it hit Bob.

_____

_____

_____

_____

_____

_____

_____

_____

_____

_____

_____

_____

_____

_____

_____

_____

Simulated Blood Drop Samples

Sample 1	Sample 2

Sample 3	Sample 4

Sample 5	Sample 6

Sample 7	Sample 8

Forensic Science Test
Teacher Instructions

Objective:

The student will take a final test over the forensic science topics covered in this book to measure his level of understanding of the procedures and processes used in evaluating a crime scene and in analyzing various types of evidence.

Gathering Materials:

A metric ruler, a calculator, a highlighter, and a trigonometric chart are needed for students to complete this test. You also will need student copies of the test on pages 130–135.

Name:_____ **Date:**_____

Forensic Science Test

Part I. Identify the following fingerprints as an arch, a loop, or a whorl.

1. _____ 2. _____ 3. _____

  (whorl print)

Part II. Match the following prints:

_____4. _____5. _____6.

A. B. C.

 (loop print B)

Part III. Using a yellow marker or highlighter, mark the following characteristics of a fingerprint. Draw a line from the marking and then write the name of the characteristic off to the side of the print. You should find and identify one of each type of characteristic.

7. Fork
8. Dot
9. Ending Ridge
10. Enclosure
11. Short Ridge

Part IV. Examine the glass fracture pattern and answer the questions.

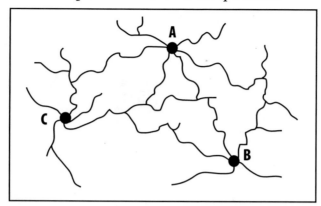

12. Which bullet was fired first?

_____

13. Which bullet was fired last?

_____

Part V. A fibula measuring 30 centimeters was found in the woods. Forensic anthropologists are trying to determine the height of the person to whom the bone belongs. Using the formulas listed below, identify how tall the person would be if the person were a male or female. Give the answers in feet and inches. Show your work and label your answer.

14. Male (fibula × 2.44) + 78.36

15. Female (fibula × 2.71) + 65.26

Part VI.   Using the blood spatter patterns below, determine the approximate angle of impact to the nearest degree. Show your work.

_____16.   _____17.

Part VII.   As a handwriting expert you are called upon to examine the following sample of writing. Choose 3 of the 12 handwriting characteristics and analyze the handwriting. Describe how each one is unique as it appears in the handwriting sample. Record your answers in the table provided.

> This is a stick up. Put all of your money in a brown paper bag. Do not hit the panic button. Follow my directions and no one will get hurt.

Handwriting Characteristic	Description of How It Appears in the Sample
18.	
19.	
20.	

Part VIII. Answer the following questions in complete sentences.

21. What type of fingerprint (arch, loop, or whorl) is the most common?

    _____

22. What type of fingerprint is the least common?

    _____

23. You are the first detective to arrive at the scene of a bank robbery. What are the five basic things you will do to properly process the crime scene?

    _____

    _____

    _____

24. What are the three methods used to process latent fingerprints?

    _____

    _____

    _____

25. Investigators suspect that a will was altered and want to process it for fingerprints. What is the best fingerprint recovery method to use when processing fingerprints on a piece of paper? Explain why.

    _____

    _____

    _____

    _____

    _____

26. Explain why fingerprints are left behind on surfaces.

_____

_____

_____

27. A small piece of fabric was recovered from a fence surrounding private property. Police suspect that the fabric swatch might provide clues to the person who illegally climbed over the fence and entered the private property. Describe the test that scientists might perform to identify the type of fabric and tell how scientists can use the results from the test to identify the fabric.

_____

_____

_____

_____

_____

28. A blood shedding event has taken place during a crime. At the scene, police notice blood spatter on a back wall. Why is the shape of the blood spatter important and how might it help police in recreating the crime?

_____

_____

_____

_____

_____

29. When forensic scientists examine evidence they look at both the physical and chemical properties. Describe the difference between physical and chemical properties, giving at least one example of each.

_____

_____

_____

_____

_____

30. You are a business owner and a customer writes a check for more than $500. You want to be sure the check is a legitimate check and not a counterfeit. Name and describe three safety features or characteristics that you could look for on the check to make sure it is genuine.

_____

_____

_____

_____

_____

Reference Materials

Books

Bell, S. (2004). *The facts on file dictionary of forensic science*. New York: Checkmark Books.

Cook, N. (1995). *Classifying fingerprints*. Parsippany, NJ: Dale Seymour Publications.

Jackson, D. (1996). *The bone detectives: How forensic anthropologists solve crimes and uncover mysteries of the dead*. Boston: Little, Brown & Company.

Owen, D. (2002). *Police lab: How forensic science tracks down and convicts criminals*. Buffalo, NY: Firefly Books Ltd.

Platt, R. (2005). *Crime scene: The ultimate guide to forensic science*. New York: Dorling Kindersley.

Platt, R. (2005). *Forensics*. Boston: Kingfisher Knowledge.

Sheely, R. (1993). *Police lab: Using science to solve crimes*. New York: Silver Moon Press.

Thomas, P. (1995). *Talking bones: The science of forensic anthropology*. New York: Facts On File.

Forensic Science Supplemental Materials

Carolina Biological Supply Company
1-800-334-5551
http://www.carolina.com

WARD'S Natural Science Company
1-800-962-2660
http://www.wardsci.com

Note: Both Carolina Biological Supply Company and WARD'S have a variety of forensic science materials, such as simulated blood, fingerprinting powder, and simulated bones, that are designed for classroom use.

Kinderprint
1-800-227-6020
http://www.kinderprint.com

Lightening Powder Company
1-800-852-0300
http://www.redwop.com

Lynn Peavey Company
1-800-255-6499
http://www.lynnpeavey.com

Note: Kinderprint, Lightening Powder, and Lynn Peavey are companies that specialize in forensic science and crime scene investigation products and equipment for law enforcement agencies and laboratories.

Answer Key

I Spy: Documenting the Crime Scene

Answers will vary.

Tool Time: Tool Impression Lab

The correct answer will depend on the screwdrivers you used. In each box students should sketch the head of the screwdriver, marking unique lines and including measurements of at least two places. They should include a written explanation also. See sample:

This screwdriver head contains horizontal lines that are thin and evenly spaced. At the widest point the head is 10 mm and at the narrowest point it is 6 mm.

Crummy Cake Chemistry: Chemical Analysis Lab

Mystery Powder 1 is flour, Mystery Powder 2 is baking soda, and Mystery Powder 3 is cornstarch. Allison is the prime suspect in the case because she owned the vial containing the baking soda. The content of her vial was a silky, fine, bright white powder. When mixed with water it turned the water a milky white and after time a residue was left at the bottom of the cup. When exposed to vinegar the powder in her vial fizzed, foamed, and bubbled up. These test results match the description of the known substance of baking soda.

Check It Out: Counterfeit Check Lab

1. Answers may vary. The perforation will feel bumpy or jagged.

2. The purpose of laid lines is to make it hard to align the parts of a check correctly after alteration by cutting and pasting.

3. Answers will vary.

4. The white spot appears because this area of the check was erased.

5. When viewed under normal lighting conditions, the appearance of the magnetic ink (the numbers) would be dull or flat.

6. Answers will vary but may include microprinting on signature line, "checksafe" logo on back, erasure protection, etc.

7. There is no perforation because none of the sides feel bumpy or jagged. This means the check was not torn from a checkbook and that it might be a counterfeit.

8. The signature line is blurry and the microprinting cannot be seen.

9. When viewed under normal lighting conditions, the appearance of the magnetic ink (the numbers) is shiny.

10. The background is blurry and laid lines are not easily seen.

Case Closed

Answers will vary. Some possible answers include information on perforations, magnetic ink, microprinting on the signature line, laid lines, etc.

Take a Bite Out of Crime: Dental Impressions Lab

Answers will vary.

Burn, Baby, Burn: Fiber Identification Lab

Answers will vary depending on the types of fabrics you choose. Cotton was found at the crime scene, so the sample that is designated cotton will belong to the guilty party.

Arches, Loops, and Whorls of Fun: Fingerprint Labs

Fingerprint Lab 1: Classifying Fingerprints
Fingerprint Identification Practice Sheet

Case Closed

Mrs. Ahren's fingerprint matches the print left behind on the door handle.

Part I.

1. loop, 2. whorl, 3. arch, 4. arch, 5. loop, 6. loop, 7. whorl, 8. whorl, 9. arch

Part II. Answers will vary.

Fingerprint Lab 2: Dusting and Lifting Prints
Case Closed

1. A fingerprint is left behind because the ridges on your fingertips leave oils on the objects we touch.
2. When dusting a print, the dust adheres to the oils left behind and causes the print to appear.
3. Technicians must wear gloves so they do not contaminate the crime scene by smearing prints or by leaving behind their own fingerprints.
4. Answers will vary.

All Cracked Up: Glass Fracture Lab

1. Bullet B was the first shot fired because the lines radiating from B were not stopped by or did not run into any other lines.
2. Bullet C was fired last because its lines run into or are stopped by the lines coming from Bullet B and Bullet A.

Case Closed:

Based on the directions for creating the window cracks in "Setting Up the Lab," bullet B was fired first. Because ballistic experts matched the bullet hole marked as B to the bullet coming from Stan's gun, this shows that Stan fired the first shot. The bullet holes marked A and C were identified as coming from Officer Johnson's gun. These holes were not fired first because the cracks radiating from these points were stopped by other cracks. Therefore, it can be confirmed that Stan fired the first shot and Officer Johnson fired twice only after Stan fired first.

Dot Your 'I's and Cross Your 'T's: Handwriting Characteristics Lab

Answers will vary.

The Genuine Article: Handwriting Forgery Lab

Answers will vary.

Grades Gone Goofy: Altered Grades Lab
Grade Sheet Analysis Chart

Angie Iversen: changed the 20 to a 30 and the 75 to a 95.
Jim Marron: changed the 11 to 24, and the 75 to a 95.
Flash McAllister: changed the 45 to a 95.
Brooke O'Neill: changed the 10 to a 100.
Noah Stevens: changed the 39 to an 89.

Case Closed:

The following people altered the indicated grades:

Angie Iversen: Research HW and Forensics Test
Jim Marron: Research HW and Forensics Test
Flash McAllister: Outline HW
Brooke O'Neill: Outline HW
Noah Stevens: Forensic Test

The Type to Commit a Crime: Typewritten Documents Lab

Answers may vary for questions 1–7, but each should include a sketch. Suggested answers are as follows.

Experiment Procedures:

1. The "h" in the robbery note has a small flag to the left of the top of the letter. The bottom of the "h" has horizontal lines across each side. Both Christopher and Diana's samples also contain these marks. However, in Christopher's sample, the marks are more rounded, and in Diana's sample, the marks are thinner, straighter lines.

2. The "a" in the robbery note has a top that curves into and touches the middle section of the letter. The end tail of the "a" is very short and smudged-looking. The "a" in Olivia's note has a top that does not touch the middle part of the letter. The tail is longer, also. In Karen's note, the top of the "a" touches the middle section and the tail is short and smudged.

3. The bottom section of the "m" in the robbery note is closed off, so that all three legs appear connected to one another. It has a small flag at the top of the first leg. The "m" in Savannah's note also has closed-off legs that connect to one another. However, her note's "m" is smudged so that the ink from the last leg appears to run into that of the middle leg. In Ashley's sample, the bottoms of the legs on the "m" do not touch one another.

4. In the "y" in the robbery note, the bottom tail has a very rounded end. The end curves into the upper section of the letter. In addition, the top of the "y" has two flags, one on each stem, that connect to one another to form an almost straight line. In Steven's note, the tail of the "y" curves out, then up. The end of the tail is not as rounded and the type is thinner. The top of the "y" has flags, but they do not touch one another. In Glenn's sample, the "y" also has a tail that curves out and up, with a slightly rounded end. The flags on the top are very small and do not touch.

5. The apostrophe in the robbery note is triangular in shape, pointing straight up and down, with the thicker section toward the top. It does have a slight flaw in the triangle, making the sides of the triangle a little uneven (it dips in a bit). This does not match the apostrophe in the following samples: Olivia, Savannah, Ashley, Diana, and Gerry.

6. The "T" in the robbery note has a distinct top with arms that point downward. The arms are very thick. The bottom of the "T" has a slightly crooked line, whose right side is thicker than the right. The middle stem of the "T" is thick toward the bottom and thin toward the top. Although all of the "T" characters in the samples contain the top arms and bottom line, looking at thickness definitely rules out Olivia, Ashley, Steven, Diana,

and Glenn. Gerry's T is too straight, so he can definitely be eliminated as well.

Case Closed

The print from the typewriter found in Karen's house matched that of the note used in the bank robbery. Therefore, it is likely that Karen is the guilty party. (*Note:* The letters "s" and "f" of Karen's sample were very distinct, as was the apostrophe. These elements, along with the varying thicknesses of the fonts should point to Karen's note as matching that of the robbery note.)

Think Ink: Ink Chromatography Lab

Answers may vary depending on which marker you used to write the ransom note. If you used the Crayola marker for the ransom note, then the person who was assigned the Crayola marker will be responsible for dognapping Matthew's prize dog.

If The Shoe Fits: Shoe Print Impression Lab

Answers will vary.

Talking Bones: Forensic Anthropology Lab

Optional Quiz:

1.C; 2. H; 3. I; 4. B; 5. N; 6. 0; 7. Q; 8. F; 9. M; 10. S; 11. L; 12. P; 13. G; 14. A; 15. J; 16. D; 17. R; 18. E; 19. K; 20. L

Experiment 1:

6.

Humerus = 40 cm

Male	Female
(H × 2.99) + 72.42	(H × 3.22) + 61.32
(40 × 2.99) + 72.42 =	(40 × 3.22) + 61.32 =
119.6 + 72.42 =	128.8 + 61.32 =
192.02 cm	190.12 cm
192.02 ÷ 2.54 ≈ 76 in.	190.12 ÷ 2.54 ≈ 75 in.
76 ÷ 12 = 6 R 4	75 ÷ 12 = 6 R 3
6 ft 4 in.	6 ft 3 in.

Fibula = 35 cm

Male	Female
$(F \times 2.44) + 78.36$	$(F \times 2.71) + 65.26$
$(35 \times 2.44) + 78.36 =$	$(35 \times 2.71) + 65.26 =$
$85.4 + 78.36 =$	$94.85 + 65.26 =$
163.76 cm	160.11 cm
$163.76 \div 2.54 \approx 64$ in.	$160.11 \div 2.54 \approx 63$ in.
$64 \div 12 = 5$ R 4	$63 \div 12 = 5$ R 3
5 ft 4 in.	5 ft 3 in.

3.

Tibia

Male	Female
$(T \times 2.37) + 80.97$	$(T \times 2.68) + 65.63$
$(22 \times 2.37) + 80.97 =$	$(22 \times 2.68) + 65.63 =$
$52.14 + 80.97 =$	$58.96 + 65.63 =$
133.11 cm	124.59 cm
$133.11 \div 2.54 \approx 52$ in.	$124.59 \div 2.54 \approx 49$ in
$52 \div 12 = 4$ R 4	$49 \div 12 = 4$ R 1
4 ft 4 in.	4 ft 1 in.

Case Closed:

The humerus could belong to a male approximately 6 feet 4 inches tall or a female 6 feet 3 inches tall. Out of the four reported missing persons only Ryan Wegener, at 6 feet 3 inches, is a close match. Therefore, the humerus might belong to Ryan.

The fibula could belong to a male approximately 5 feet 4 inches tall or a female 5 feet 3 inches tall. Out of the four reported missing persons only Cheryl Hartmann, at 5 feet 3 inches, is a match. Therefore, the fibula might belong to Cheryl.

Experiment 2:

(Answers are given for the pictures of the bones found on page 110–111.)

1. A. Humerus bone (to the nearest centimeter): 25 cm

B. Tibia bone (to the nearest centimeter): 22 cm

2.

Humerus

Male	Female
$(H \times 2.99) + 72.42$	$(H \times 3.22) + 61.32$
$(25 \times 2.99) + 72.42 =$	$(25 \times 3.22) + 61.32 =$
$74.75 + 72.42 =$	$80.5 + 61.32 =$
147.17 cm	141.82 cm
$147.17 \div 2.54 \approx 58$ in.	$141.82 \div 2.54 \approx 56$ in.
$58 \div 12 = 4$ R 10	$56 \div 12 = 4$ R 8
4 ft 10 in.	4 ft 8 in.

Case Closed:

The bones could not belong to the same person. If the person was a male, the length of the humerus indicates a male 4 feet 10 inches tall, but the length of the tibia suggests a male 4 feet 4 inches tall. If the person was a female, the length of the humerus indicates a female 4 feet 8 inches tall, but the length of the tibia suggests a female 4 feet 1 inch tall.

Seeing Red: Blood Spatter Labs

Lab 1: Surface-Shape Relationship

Type of Surface	Porous or Nonporous	Sketch of Blood Spatter
Carpet Square	Porous	jagged edges
Glass	Nonporous	smooth edges
Ceramic Tile	Nonporous	smooth edges
Cardboard	Porous	jagged edges
Fabric	Porous	jagged edges
Sponge	Porous	jagged edges

Note: Appearance of blood spatter may vary. The type of edge expected for each type of surface is indicated in the third column.

Case Closed

The plastic CD case and the hood of a car are both nonporous surfaces, so the blood spatter would have smooth edges. A sidewalk, a newspaper, and a paper towel are all porous surfaces, so any blood hitting those surfaces would have jagged edges.

Lab 2: Distance-Shape Relationship

6. Answers will vary.

7. The size of the blood spatter got larger as the height from which the blood dropped increased.

8. Although the size of the blood spatter increased, the shape of the blood spatter remained the same. All four shapes were oval in design.

Case Closed:

Answers may vary. Possible answer: I would testify in court that Sam was not close to the wall when he was shot. The blood spatter is large and therefore indicates that the impact was not made at a close range. I would support Sam's story, which states that he was standing about 4 feet away from the wall when he was shot. Because the blood spatter was large in size, the impact was made from a distance.

Lab 3: Angle of Impact

Note. Answers may vary slightly according to student measurement.

Sample Number	Width (in mm)	Length (in mm)	Ratio (as a decimal)	Angle of Impact in Degrees
1.	10	24	.4166	25
2.	18	29	.6206	38
3.	25	27	.9259	68
4.	5	33	.1515	9
5.	18	20	.91	64
6.	20	24	.8333	56
7.	14	25	.56	34
8.	20	20	1.0	90

Case Closed:

Bob is telling the truth. If the blood spatter is circular in shape, it indicates the angle of impact is around 90°, which means Bob and Rob had to be standing at the same level when the shot was fired. If Rob fired the gun when he was lying on the floor, the gun would have been angled up and the resulting blood spatter would have been long and thin in shape.

Forensic Science Test

Part I.
1. whorl; 2. arch; 3. loop

Part II.
4. C; 5. A; 6. B.

Part III.
7–11. Answers will vary.

Part IV.
12. C; 13. B

Part V.
14. Approximately 5 feet; 15. Approximately 4 feet 10 inches

Part VI.
16. approximately 9°; 17. approximately 49°

Part VII.
18–20. Answers will vary.

Part VIII.

21. A loop is the most common type of fingerprint.

22. An arch is the least common type of fingerprint.

23. The first thing I would do is check the victim if there was one. I would then secure the area using special police tape. After that I would document the area by taking pictures or making sketches. I would then search the area looking for and gathering evidence and finally I would interview any witnesses.

24. The three methods used to process latent fingerprints are dusting, superglue fuming, and using ninhydrin.

25. The best method to use on paper is ninhydrin because the ninhydrin will stain the prints, allowing them to last indefinitely. It is not possible to "lift" a print from paper using the dusting method.

26. Fingerprints are left behind because our fingertips are made up of tiny ridges. These ridges contain oils and when we touch a surface those oils are left behind. When we then dust the surface, the dust adheres to the oils making the prints visible.

27. A test that might be performed is a burn test. Scientists take a sample of the fabric and expose it to a flame. Different fabrics will react in different ways. Some will burn immediately and some may just melt or curl up. Scientists will compare the results of the burn test from the unknown sample to that of a known sample to identify the fabric.

28. The shape of the blood spatter is important because it can tell the angle at which the impact of the blood shedding event occurred. Police can use this information to reconstruct a crime scene. For example, if the blood spatter is long and thin in shape, the angle of impact may have occurred at an acute angle like 20°. If the blood spatter is round in shape, the impact occurred closer to a 90° angle. Using this information, police can determine where someone was standing or positioned when he was hit or shot.

29. Physical properties describe the evidence as it occurs without coming into contact with any other substance. Examples of a physical property are the color, texture, or smell of a substance. Chemical properties are used to describe the effects of the evidence coming into contact with something else. For example, when baking soda is exposed to vinegar, it fizzes, foams, and bubbles up.

30. Answers will vary. Some possibilities: microprinting on the signature line, perforations, appearance of magnetic ink, laid lines, safety features listed on the back of the check, or white marks appearing as the result of chemical protection.

About the Author

Karen K. Schulz received her bachelor's degree in elementary education and mathematics from Southern Illinois University at Carbondale in 1984. She received a master of arts in teaching from Webster University in 1989. In 1996, she earned her gifted certification from Webster University. She currently teaches at Wildwood Middle School in the Rockwood School District. Karen has been teaching middle school gifted education since 1993. Prior to teaching gifted education she taught mathematics.

Over the years, Karen has presented her forensic science curriculum at numerous gifted education conferences. In 2001, Karen received the national "Education's Unsung Hero Award" from ING Northern Annuity for her work in developing a forensic science curriculum for her classroom. In the fall of 2005, she won a national competition sponsored by Olympus America and Tool Factory, for her continuing work with forensics in the classroom.

Karen creates much of her own curriculum. Recognizing that there was a lack of quality materials available in the area of forensics, Karen developed the simulation and storylines that were published as *Crime Scene Detective, Crime Scene Detective: Arson,* and *Crime Scene Detective: Theft. CSI Expert!: Forensic Science for Kids* is Karen's fourth book on forensic science materials for the classroom.

Karen lives in Ballwin, MO, with her husband Jim, their daughter Taylor, and their son Matthew.